Kim Izzo is the arts/features director at *Flare* magazine. She has been a frequent contributor to various newspapers and magazines including *The Globe and Mail* (Canada's national newspaper), *Style* and *Fashion* magazine.

Ceri Marsh is editor-in-chief of *Fashion* magazine and editorial director of *Fashion18* magazine. Her articles have appeared frequently in *The Globe and Mail* newspaper, *Toronto Life* magazine and *Flare* magazine.

Izzo and Marsh's first book together, *The Fabulous Girl's Guide to Decorum*, is also published by Corgi.

Also by Kim Izzo and Ceri Marsh

THE FABULOUS GIRL'S GUIDE TO DECORUM

and published by Corgi Books

Kim Izzo and Ceri Marsh

The Fabulous Girl's Guide to Life

CORGI BOOKS

THE FABULOUS GIRL'S GUIDE TO LIFE
A CORGI BOOK : 0 552 15069 X

First publication in Great Britain
Originally published in Canada by Anchor Canada under the title
The Fabulous Girl's Code Red

PRINTING HISTORY
Corgi edition published 2004

1 3 5 7 9 10 8 6 4 2

Set in Garamond by
Falcon Oast Graphic Art Ltd.

Corgi Books are published by Transworld Publishers,
61–63 Uxbridge Road, London W5 5SA,
a division of The Random House Group Ltd,
in Australia by Random House Australia (Pty) Ltd,
20 Alfred Street, Milsons Point, Sydney, NSW 2061, Australia,
in New Zealand by Random House New Zealand Ltd,
18 Poland Road, Glenfield, Auckland 10, New Zealand
and in South Africa by Random House (Pty) Ltd,
Endulini, 5a Jubilee Road, Parktown 2193, South Africa.

Printed and bound in Great Britain by
Cox & Wyman Ltd, Reading, Berkshire.

Papers used by Transworld Publishers are natural, recyclable products
made from wood grown in sustainable forests. The manufacturing processes
conform to the environmental regulations of the country of origin.

To Meredyth

Contents

CONTENTS

Introduction

Two wise women once said that manners make you sexy. Oh, yeah, that was us. In our first book, *The Fabulous Girl's Guide to Decorum*, we set out to create a primer for women who crave both civility and style. We wanted to declare that far from making you a retiring bore, manners will make you a better and more socially desirable person.

In our own lives, there were so many women of great charm, wit and decorum that we wanted to celebrate the type: the Fabulous Girl. FG to her friends. She's that stylish, witty and caring friend you rely on to make parties more fun and disappointments less painful. She is not interested in the road of bad behaviour, which is so much more travelled. She chooses to set off down another path, that of civility. The FG knows how to get the most out of life while still remaining a caring part of her society.

But it's hard. Everyday we all encounter countless acts of selfishness and bad behaviour. Whether it's a friend who is always late, a mate who forgets to introduce you at parties, the stranger who cuts you off on the road or a colleague who takes credit for your work, etiquette is at an all-time low. The erosion of etiquette and civility over the past several decades is regrettable. At a time when we so desperately need civility, we find an intense focus on personal satisfaction in its place. Although bad manners are not appealing, they are increasingly common. And who wants to be common?

Not the FG. Rather than become cynical as a result of the rude old world she lives in, she rallies to the cause of decorum. The Fabulous Girl is passionate. She may be well mannered, but she is never mild mannered. Her zest for life is one of her most charming attributes. It also means she finds herself in extreme situations. Despite the best-laid plans (or because of the best-laid plans), sometimes life spins out of control. An FG does not live to avoid these sorts of adventures. In love and work and in her friendships, the FG throws herself in deep – which can bring her big success as well as, sometimes, big disappointments. The FG knows that her word to live by is 'decorum,' not 'doormat,' so she tackles these ups and downs with equal vigour. She defines for herself what it means to have it all, and she looks for balance among the jumble of responsibilities and relationships that make up her life. An FG never shies away from this challenge. She knows that these adventures are the very fabric of her great big life.

The Fabulous Girl's Guide to Life is geared toward this very Fabulous Girl. The one who uses her style and social decorum to cope with life's inevitable rollercoaster ride. We can all behave beautifully when things are going our way, can't we? But an FG wants to maintain her grace even under extreme circumstances. Some crises and turning points will come as a result of her evolving life – big jobs, big relationships – and some crazy and uncomfortable moments – cash windfalls, getting fired, discovering a philandering spouse –

will arise in ways that are beyond her control. These are the moments that really count – when it's hard, when you'd rather be selfish or rude than extend yourself for another person, when you just feel like stamping your little foot – and they are true tests of character. But it is this ability to behave with grace under pressure, as well as her style, manners and wit, that sets the Fabulous Girl apart and, yes, makes her sexy.

CHAPTER ONE

The Workplace

'What did you do to your hair? It looks good.'
Cheryl, a senior editor at *Smack!* Magazine, squealed at me
as she ran past my desk. Despite the backhanded
compliment, I had to admit that I was having an unusually
good hair day. Normally my hair misbehaves a few times a
week, generally when I have a can't-miss cocktail party to
attend. But that day my tresses looked fab. I chose to take
my good hair as an omen for the rest of the day.

I loved my job as associate editor for the magazine.
Smack! is known in the rag trade as a general-interest
magazine, but I'd been hired to give it specific interest:
young and hip. In other words, it was my job to tell our
middle-aged readership about what the pretty young things
were drinking and shopping for, where they went to listen
to music and get their hair done. I'd been at it for over a
year. And while I was happy, I was beginning to want to
move my work in another direction – upwards, that is – but
unfortunately I couldn't yet grasp what exactly where up
was.

Whack! Something walloped my desk with a mighty slap.

'Do you read Dudley's page?'

There stood John Bradley, *Smack!*'s editor-in-chief, the big
boss, with a wad of rolled-up newspaper in his hand. I
wondered if he was now going to swat me on the nose with it.

'He's funny. Your writing should be more like his. You know, chatty.'

'But he's a gossip columnist.'

'And?'

'And I'm not.' I tried not to sound annoyed, but lately Bradley seemed to find fault in whatever I did or didn't do.

'Well, if you'd rather have dull copy. Did you dye your hair?'

'No, it's just a good—'

Bradley hurried away leaving the offending paper on my desk. Dudley's gossip column ran in a national newspaper. Since being on the job, I'd become an observer of sorts. Being out many nights a week gave me lots of opportunity to people watch. I'd met Dudley on many occasions and he was not what you'd call gentlemanly. I wasn't really on his radar – he would barely say hello to me. And now there was Dudley's sucky face sneering at me.

Truth be told, I hated his column. It was brash, tacky and rude. He was not the sort of gossip columnist who lived to suck up to local celebrities, he was the kind of creep who wormed his way into parties thrown by the well-known only to turn around and mock their choice of wine or fashion sense in his next column. But like the dutiful worker bee, I read Dudley's words, most of it meaningless drivel. Meaningless, that is, until I got to the last paragraph, which was horrifying: 'TV producer Bingo Jones was all hot and bothered with local celeb news babe Mel (first name only please) at last night's opening of the so-hip-it-hurts eaterie Spanks. If Bingo's regular chica, mag art director Eleanor Brown, had eye-spied the duo giving each other a good tongue lashing, it would have been spanks all right.'

Now, I've never been a fan of Bingo. He was an ill-mannered lout, the kind of guy who took mobile calls at dinner parties, was rude to waitresses and, worse, was a terrible boyfriend. I knew this last fact to be utterly true because Bingo was in a long-term relationship, off and on, off and on, with my best friend Eleanor. And the fact that Bingo was now a confirmed cheating bastard (during a supposed 'on' moment) really riled me. As did Eleanor's public humiliation at the keyboard of Dudley.

My first reaction? Poor Eleanor! My second – I would never stoop to those depths in my writing! Bradley would have to find another writer to dish the dirt. The fact that I wanted to keep my job, however, prevented me from marching into his office to tell him so. I was hoping he'd just forget the entire conversation and continue with his latest idea for making over *Smack!*, which was more sex and gardening.

But first and foremost, I had to reach Eleanor. She would need her friends. I called her work, her home and her mobile. No answer. Which meant one thing: Eleanor had read Dudley's column. There was only one other person who might have known her whereabouts, our other best friend, Missy. I dialled.

'She's here.'

I must admit Missy's revelation caught me off guard. Sure, we're all equally close, but I was mystified as to why Eleanor would choose refuge in the suburbs over me. Why was Missy her first call?

Let me explain something: Missy lived on the outskirts of the city. In a very big house, 3500 square feet, 60-foot lot with a four-car garage. But Missy didn't drive. Her husband, Joe, had struck it super rich and Missy was still adjusting to her new-found wealth. This was becoming a bit of an issue with me. Along with the fatter wallet came a fatter head. In any case, it had taken a lot of effort for Eleanor to get to Missy. I was a mere bike ride away.

'Eleanor doesn't want to talk right now. Can she call you later?' sighed Missy.

I hung up the phone, still unsure of why Eleanor didn't want to talk to me and further irked by Missy's tone.

'Did you change your hair?'

The question shook me out of my pondering. I contemplated shaving my head. A few more of my colleagues hovered around my desk.

'Just a good hair day.'

Bradley hussled over with his coat on. 'We're all going to lunch, want to join us?'

I was dumbfounded. I mean, never once since my first *Smack!* day had I been invited to one of Bradley's lunch things. Naturally, I couldn't say no, no matter how ticked I still was at the Dudley incident – perhaps I was finally being let into the inner circle of senior editors. Don't get me wrong, people have been nice to me, but seeing as I'm so junior, the so-called real journalists had kind of kept their distance from me. I knew that they considered my pages the necessary but shallow fluff that kept advertisers happy. My out-and-about pages and the fashion and décor pages were the fluffy ghetto of the magazine. But then, an invitation to lunch. This was serious. We all headed out to Bradley's regular café. Although my mind kept obsessing about Eleanor, I tried to fit in with the group.

'We have to get that piece on John Daly in before next week.'

'Who's John Daly?'

Bradley looked at me like I had asked him how to spell my own name.

'Um, he's probably going to be elected mayor,' said Cheryl.

'Oh, that John Daly!' I lied.

For the rest of the walk to lunch I tried not to feel excluded from the conversation, but I was afraid to say anything else. I was positive that they were questioning

Bradley's judgment in hiring me, let alone inviting me. I consoled myself with the knowledge that I was at the very least charming and I vowed to be bright and witty at lunch.

Arriving at the restaurant we were led to a large round table and began to fan out. I walked around the entire circumference and ended up sandwiched between Cheryl and the arts writer, Marshall, with big boss Bradley straight across from me.

We ordered. I assumed Bradley was picking up the tab and so went for a slightly larger lunch than I would normally have. Besides, half the table were eating steak so my salmon wasn't the end of the world. But still, I was too intimidated to speak.

'I was thinking of giving the movie roundup piece to Stella,' Marshall announced.

Bradley simply nodded. There was only one film critic in town named Stella, Stella DuBois, and I thought she was dreadful. She hated everything she saw, and her writing was grossly self-indulgent. Every review she wrote somehow came back to her and some formative experience in her life. Finally, a topic I could get in on.

'No, you're not giving work to that hack?'

Marshall just looked at me in disbelief. I took this as a sign that few people challenged him, but I was aiming to prove I could hold my own in this merry group. I'd show Bradley I was no dummy.

'I mean she hates everything, but has no critical eye. I read that she once tried to make a film but her script was so bad no one would touch it. She's just a frustrated filmmaker who takes her own disappointment out on the real artists. And don't get me started on her writing!'

I had never seen people so silent. Cheryl and Marshall smiled meekly. Everyone else stared down at their plates. Everyone except Bradley.

'She happens to be my wife,' Bradley announced, not looking up at me as he stabbed his steak and tore it apart.

I wanted to quietly swallow my own head. How had I not known this? I mean, sure, Bradley kept to himself, and I was hardly his confidante, but no one had ever mentioned Stella and Bradley in the same sentence. I had a vague memory of seeing Stella at the Christmas party, but she had drunk too much and left early.

'I'm so sorry, I had no idea.'

'They like to keep their personal lives private. You couldn't have known, only industry types would know.' Marshall tried to make me feel better, but I was stung by the implication that I wasn't even in the same industry as the rest of them. It didn't really matter what I said now, my stiletto was in my big mouth and deep down I knew my days at *Smack!* were numbered. There would be no upward mobility for me. I finished my salmon in silence.

Back at my desk, I listened to my voice mail, trying to recover from the lunch debacle by being busy, too busy to listen to my colleagues' whispered comments. Most of my messages were from PR people pushing products that were of no interest to me. I dubbed these annoying phone calls, 'sevens,' the number I pressed on my phone's keypad to erase them. This was also true of mean and nasty reader calls. 'What do you know about a good bar? I read your piece on Dino's last month and you suck. It's the best place. My brother-in-law owns it so I know it's good. I think you should be standing under a cliff during an avalanche.' Definitely a seven. But not a single call from Eleanor. I looked at the clock: 4:57 P.M. I was so glad it was quitting time. Despite my sunny outlook at 9 A.M., I was feeling deflated. I looked in my compact mirror, even my hair had become limp. So much for having a good hair day.

Fabulous Girl as Big Girl

Finally, after years of Jill Jobs, those 'nowhere jobs' most of us start out with, the FG has made it. She's got to where she wants to be, or at least a lot closer than that temp job was. The Fabulous Girl with a career has to navigate a whole new professional landscape. Work is still one of her highest priorities and where she spends most of her time and mental energy. But if she's lucky, she's spending it doing something she loves. As a wise FG once said, 'Find a job you love and you'll never work a day in your life.'

In the early days of her career, a young woman's burdens are most likely to be boredom and frustration. She may feel stuck with tasks that she feels are beneath her abilities. As her work life takes off she'll have different pressures: keeping up a level of performance she has established for herself, the added responsibilities of her seniority. Even an FG at the top of her professional game can have a Bad Hair Day or a Fat Day. And while the FG thinks these are prime reasons to call in sick, her boss probably won't. But for truly bad days, the FG may have to pull out all the tools in her decorum arsenal or else risk turning into the angry, bitter, depressed type she shrinks from.

Fabulous Work Space

TEAMWORK

Assembly lines aren't exclusive to factories churning out widgets. In past decades the standard office environment consisted of row upon row of uniform desks and chairs situated in one large room. If that seems barbaric to the

Fabulous Girl aesthetic, consider the current equivalent for cost-cutters in the corporate world – the open-plan work-space. Here the 'cubicle dwellers' sit at their desks toiling away at their jobs. Love them or hate them, the little cubes are here to stay. For the FG stuck in cube country, however, there are ways of coping with grace.

Privacy

You really don't have any, do you? Staunch supporters of cube country suggest that what the cubicles lack in privacy they make up for in team building. Collaboration, it seems, is easier when you don't have to waste precious seconds picking up a phone or strolling to someone else's office to speak with them. Hey, we thought that's what boardrooms and luncheons were for. Apparently it is downright inspiring to have colleagues overhear your sales pitch or see what your presentation looks like on your computer screen so they can give you their two pennies' worth without your needing to ask. How convenient. However, what all cube-country residents need to understand is that just because you don't have any privacy doesn't mean you shouldn't respect the illusion of it. Don't give your opinion on your colleagues' work unless you're asked for it; they may not be ready to share their work yet and may resent you butting in. Likewise for personal problems. If you hear Sue fighting with her boyfriend, you cannot say, 'So sorry you're having problems, do you need to talk about it?' Pretend you heard nothing! Sue will confide if and when she wants to.

Did you hear that?

A voice that is obviously speaking quietly is one that wants to avoid detection. Take this as a sign to distract yourself with something else, say, your own work. And while no one really wants to hear you whisper sweet nothings to your accountant, sometimes it cannot be helped. If a call is very private then it's time to take your mobile to the car park or use a boardroom phone instead.

Why shout? No matter how eager you are to express your enthusiasm to a new client over the phone, raised voices are very distracting to your colleagues in cube country. If you sense colleagues stuffing cotton into their ears, turning up their desk radios or sneering at you, then take these hints to pipe down.

Other distractions

As you might with a noisy neighbour, sometimes you may have to address a colleague's habits in order to carry on with your own work. If you are slaving over this month's bottom line but your cube buddies spend all day talking about Saturday night plans, then feel free to bring it up with them. Chances are, they weren't aware that you could hear them and this reminder will embarrass them enough to keep it down – and they may also be a bit worried that you'll squeal to the boss about their work ethic. Either way, the problem should be solved. Music is nice, but not everyone will appreciate your love of opera or Eminem. Really, boom boxes and radios shouldn't be played without headphones.

Desk hovering

Just because there aren't any doors on the darn things doesn't mean it's all open concept all the time. If your team-mate is on the phone or eating her lunch, you cannot just stand there in her tiny space waiting for her to finish so that you can talk to her. Come back when she's free. At best, stick a Post-it down to inform her of what you need and she'll find you when it's a better time.

The People in Your Workspace

BOYS WILL BE BOYS

Some types of work environments are still dominated by men. The FG does not try to be 'one of the guys.' She relishes her femininity, and since she acts with grace the men around her will respond in kind. However, if you are the sole female in a workplace then you can expect the men to be on their guard. And that's just fine with an FG. She has no problem being a civilizing presence. Hopefully, the guys will take into account that an FG doesn't want to listen to PMS jokes or constant sports talk (unless she's in a sporting field). If one or two gents seem to be behaving in an ungentlemanly fashion, the FG would initially much rather deal with the issue on her own, perhaps asking the guilty party to refrain from his off-colour humour or constant belching, with subtlety first: 'You really should stop eating that chilli every-day, Bob.' Fortunately, most men are acutely aware of the PC attitudes that permeate the modern workplace and will be hyper-aware of potential problems.

If the man or men do not co-operate after her polite request but continue in a loutish mode, the FG should stand her ground and give fair warning. Tell him or them explicitly to quit with the sexist comments or to remove the centrefold tacked up in the lunchroom. If this doesn't work, an FG will need to take it up with her manager. Of course, if bad behaviour turns into out-and-out harassment, then there are other, legal courses of action.

GIRLS! GIRLS! GIRLS!

Working with women can be great. There can be great bonding and fun in an all-female workplace. And someone in the office is going to have a tampon when you get surprised by your period. The FG thrives in estrogen-strong situations, being a girly-girl herself. However, she does occasionally experience a downside. Workplaces staffed entirely by women can have the double-edge sword of surplus sensitivity. This is great when you get dumped and your chick-mates understand why you're a wreck for two weeks. But the flip side is that feelings can easily be hurt within this feminine office. You may find that you need to – or think you need to – watch your tone of voice more carefully. This can be tiring and can make jobs take longer than they should. Gossip can also be more rampant with a female majority, and again this is unavoidable, for if you don't spend some time gossiping then the other 'girls' will think you unfriendly. It's all about balance.

If an FG works in a predominantly female office where one or two men also work, the conversations need to be sensitive. That's right – male-sensitive. When women discuss bad dates or mean boyfriends, things can easily devolve into male bashing, which is very impolite. Conversely, trying to get them to explain why your boyfriend is a jerk is also not fair.

THE UNDERMINER

Great jobs are hard to come by. So when you have an awesome job, someone somewhere wants to take it away from you. It could be your assistant, or even a colleague with a similar job. But you notice that this person tries to 'help' you out with your projects when you don't even ask for assistance. The FG will spot underminers by these signs:

1. They offer to go to that meeting or industry event so you can take a much-needed night off.

2. You discuss how a task is to be done, but by the

deadline they've done it an entirely different way without bothering to tell you until presentation time.

3. They've made contacts on your behalf but haven't passed them along to you.

4. They tell your boss how much they've done on your project because you're too busy.

5. They commit to helping you out but bail at the last minute knowing you don't have enough time to complete the job.

Once the Fabulous Girl has spotted an Underminer, she needs to take action. Since this person can no longer be trusted the FG needs to prevent her from being closely involved in the FG's work. She'll need to avoid working on projects with the Underminer, but also avoid her at work-related social events. The Fabulous Girl should also be more aggressive in the presence of the Underminer, never allowing this person to take over a project or to represent the FG's work in a meeting. The one thing the FG wants to avoid is being seen as paranoid. This can be achieved by not running to the boss or other colleagues and spilling her guts and woes. She needs to handle the Underminer alone, like a lone sheriff in an old western film.

THE SUCK-UP

This person kisses your boss's arse at every opportunity, even if it means insulting or undermining colleagues. The Suck-Up will pass the buck on his own mistakes or tell the boss how he loves an idea but behind the boss's back tell you how stupid it is. The only solace for the Fabulous Girl is that chances are the boss knows a simpering sycophant when she sees one. The FG never falls for the charms of such a person, nor does she seek favour by acting in kind.

THE INCOMPETENT

Bingo is an idiot. Everyone knows it, right? He's so obviously incompetent that it's difficult not to let your lack of respect for him show at work. But at an absolute minimum you must treat him – even behind his back – with decorum. Remember that someone hired him, and likely that person is your boss. Any slag you make against Bingo is an indirect slag against his superior. Many bosses are extremely defensive about the hires they make and will take personally any criticism of them. Most managers also have a lot of problems to solve each day, so don't make Bingo two problems. His incompetence is the first and most obvious hassle, but then your unhappiness about it becomes another. If you are in a position where you must complain about Bingo to your boss or in front of your boss, be very careful. Stick to the facts and make no personal remarks: 'I found my job difficult this month since Bingo delivered his reports three weeks late. I was able to compensate for the lost time, but it wasn't an ideal situation.' It behooves you to go out of your way to seem reasonable and accommodating when dealing with the Incompetent, as you will come off as the star of the situation. You will also do much more to change your boss's opinion of Bingo.

THE PRYER

She's friendly, a great listener, and she seems very, very interested in your personal and work life. Every time she comes near you she has a salacious titbit about someone else in the office. Which means her prodding questioning about how much overtime you put in last month isn't so she can sympathize, it's ammo to take to the next person and say, 'She's just rancid about having to work all weekend, she really thinks she's doing more than anybody.' If you've been burned by the Pryer, or see her doing it with others, then you simply must keep quiet about your opinions, especially those concerning the job and company, and make it clear to her that you're not interested in the opinions of others when she tries to share.

THE TASKMASTER

We all need a bit of a kick now and again to meet deadlines. But somehow there is always one person who sets about in a manic fashion, driving everyone else so hard that the work actually suffers. Granted, some people respond well to added pressure or being spoken to like children, but the Fabulous Girl is not one of them. She doesn't see the need to get spastic about a report that is due, she just does it. So when the Taskmaster rants and raves and tells the FG ten times that she has three days to complete her report, the FG just goes numb. It is counterproductive. The FG needs to calmly repeat to the TM that all is under control. When she sees the TM coming her way, she may cut her off at the pass by saying, 'Yes, I know it's due. Is there something else I can help you with?'

THE DISAPPROVING ASSISTANT

The qualities that make good leaders are not the same as those that make good administrators. Good leaders are usually people with vision – they are not necessarily good with details. It is often confusing for those who toil in support positions to work for leaders who are not good at coping with minutiae. In fact, an organized and efficient assistant can find her boss's haphazard way with schedules or paperwork extremely annoying. This classic role reversal can result in the assistant's developing a disapproving, tsk-tsking attitude toward her boss.

When an FG boss finds herself in this situation, she needs to address it. If an FG feels in any way guilty being in charge of someone else's time, it may be tempting to fall into this codependent relationship. It's sort of an 'I feel bad that I'm your boss, so let's both pretend that I'm incompetent without you' mode. This dangerous game can end up with the boss being pushed around by her assistant. An FG boss needs to make it clear that it does not matter a whit that she is bad about entering info into her electronic diary because that isn't her job and she is busy with the things that are. Remember, your assistant will often have more contact with the rest of the staff than you will, and so how she treats you and talks about you is important. When your whereabouts are enquired after and your assistant rolls her eyes or sighs before answering, she is undermining your authority in the workplace.

An FG may feel uncomfortable about getting tough in this situation, but she must. She's worked hard to earn her position and the right to an assistant. She may need to pull back from a pals-y relationship with her assistant, be a bit more formal to right this imbalance.

Bad Business

DISAGREEMENTS WITH COLLEAGUES

If a colleague's suggestion doesn't sit right with you, say so immediately – especially if it affects you personally. Of course, you need to express your concern in a diplomatic and controlled way: no temper tantrums. But don't assume that speaking up puts you in conflict with your colleague. Know that you are just adding information to the discussion. If Bingo's pitch to create a new department at your office means that you and everyone else in the office will end up having to work Saturdays from now on, you need to pipe up. If your objections are ignored or dismissed without proper debate, take the person or your boss aside and make your point again. Go on the record if you feel passionate about it; send a memo to the interested parties. It's possible you won't alter the course of events, but your 'told you so' moment is assured if their plans fail. And let's face it – sometimes we love to say, or at least think, those three words.

BIG BOSS ERRORS

The situation is more sensitive if the bad idea comes down from the boss. Your only recourse is to present alternatives, again on paper, and then keep quiet. If the situation becomes too ridiculous, it may be time to hit the want ads for another gig. But then, if the idea's really bad, your boss may be looking for work too.

BOSS IS BOMBING

When you got your job she was on top of the world. She was successful and her career was on an upswing. No wonder you were so enthusiastic about hitching your wagon to her star. Now things are beginning to look a little different. You can see it in *her* boss's eyes: she's on her way out. As someone closely associated with her, what do you do?

Assuming that you still respect your boss, you can do one or two things. If your boss is the talented and intelligent person whom you've always admired, it won't take much for you to stand up for her in a down time. Not necessarily covering for her, but if need be, that too. You may consider having a heart-to-heart to let her know in a subtle fashion what others may be thinking of her. Ask her what's troubling her and see if she is simply unhappy and is in fact contemplating a change of jobs.

If the situation is indeed a lost cause and you find you're on a sinking ship, it is more complicated. Although an FG is a loyal person, she needs to play this situation very carefully. How happy are you in your job? If you love your job but have to admit that your mentor isn't what she used to be and doesn't seem open to help or advice, then you need to make some strategic moves now.

1. Start distancing yourself from your lame-duck boss. Let people in your company know that you are independent.

2. Try to find out if the powers that be see the two of you as a team. If you are thought to be her right hand, then you should probably start looking for a job. The seniors in your company may never be able to think of you as a separate entity, and if your boss is replaced, her successor will certainly have a hard time getting over your relationship with your old boss.

3. If you think there's room for change, then do what you can to distinguish yourself from her. Work on solo projects. Put it out there that you did it on your own.

4. Spend some time with different people in your company.

SURVIVE A MERGER

If your company gets bought by a bigger one, then you'll be seeing the landscape change pretty quickly. Try not to get caught up in the panic that can set in during a merger. Get information. Listen to gossip. Ask for a meeting with your boss and have a frank conversation. What does she know about what is going to happen? Is your job secure? What can you do? Make sure to meet the new bosses as soon as you can. Introduce yourself and make it clear that you're excited to be working with them. This may seem simple, but it's amazing how many people don't make it through a power change because they didn't have the sense to pledge allegiance to the new regime. New bosses who are taking over an old staff often worry about the old staff's loyalties. Let your new boss know you're looking forward to working with her. Don't get involved in office gossip focusing on what your old boss did that this new fool doesn't. It almost always gets back to the new boss.

The Work

FG AS WORKHORSE

FGs hate to let others down. They are therefore easily guilted into accepting too heavy a workload. In the early years of her career, an FG may decide that she wants to make an impression on those around her by working like a demon. She will take on many tasks and complete them brilliantly, never complaining. By working hard like this, an FG is sure to gain a reputation as, well, a hard worker. She may not, however, make the move up the ladder in this way. Hard work is not always what is most prized in the professional world.

After you have paid your dues for a few years, you need to change your status from workhorse to show pony. It is time to switch strategies and be more choosy about how much work you do yourself and how much you delegate. Because that's what leaders do. They make important choices and then gather people around them to help execute their plans. So when your boss is heaping an unreasonable amount of work on you, you don't have to wimp out and say you can't do it. Instead, say that you'd love to manage all the projects she has in mind, and present her with your plan to oversee some of the work that others will do.

EVERYBODY HATES YOU

On rare occasions, an FG will find herself the object of her employees' wrath. They hate her. They don't respect her and at any opportunity they challenge her authority. When she walks into a room, conversation stops. There is eye rolling going on in meetings when she makes presentations. Despite the FG's being the boss of them, they are ruining her work environment. However, employment laws being what they are, big boss FG cannot simply hand out a fistful of P45s. She has to work with her cranky crew.

In such an extreme situation, the first thing the Fabulous Girl needs to determine is whether her staff have a legitimate reason. Was she once their colleague but in her promotion has grown bitchy and condescending toward them? Are they jealous because of the promotion, or is she simply new to the job? The FG may need to modify her own behaviour by being more reasonable if she realizes she has not been a considerate boss. But if no discernible reason exists, then the FG must learn to distinguish between personal and professional attitudes. The Fabulous Girl wants to be liked by everyone – an impossible feat even if she's not the boss. So she will have to accept that, as boss, she is bound to be disliked by some of her staff. She cannot punish a person who dislikes her in any way or treat that person differently than the others if he or she is performing the work adequately. Of course, if said person blatantly challenges her authority in front of coworkers, say by whispering to a colleague in a meeting or rolling his or her eyes at a suggestion made by the boss FG,

35

then a thorough one-on-one talking to is in order. Here the FG must be firm and put her foot down. She doesn't have to be liked, but she does have to be respected. In fact, the less the FG appears to be moved by her employee's malevolence, the more they are likely to give her respect. These scenarios are never pleasant and no one wants to toil in a tense environment, but the rotten apples may decide that they hate the FG boss so much they quit.

WORK SUPPORT: LISTEN WELL

It's one of the great myths that complainers actually want someone to fix their troubles. What's far more likely is that the complainer wants the person they're whining to to simply listen and sympathize. (This is a particularly difficult one for men to wrap their minds around.)

There she is again. Fifi is standing in your office for the umpteenth time complaining about her unappreciative boss. What to do? Most of us have been tricked into giving unwanted advice. Work troubles can be complicated because many people have ongoing problems that they may need to vent about. Passive-aggressive assistants and undermining colleagues are the kind of problems that tend to need chronic airing. As the friend of someone with a problem, you must be careful not to fall into some of these traps.

Don't give pat answers. If you've heard your friend whine about how undervalued she is in her job for the past year and a half, you understandably will want to recommend that she do something about it. Don't. Any advice that starts with 'just,' as in 'just tell your boss you're not working on the weekends and nights anymore,' will not be appreciated. It may seem clear what the answers are, but most people will be insulted if their troubles are reduced to one-line fix-ups.

Don't encourage confrontation. Workplaces are complicated

systems. Assume that you don't understand the lay of the land. Therefore, think twice before encouraging your friend to have it out with the guy who sits next to her who may be taking credit for your friend's work but also who has lunch with the boss and is more powerful than he seems.

Instead

What does she want? Ask your friend what she wants out of her bitch session – probably just a chance to vent her irritation over work troubles, and possibly some help in analyzing the psychology of the people in her office. Do not immediately assume that she is looking for you to solve her problems.

If the complainer has been upset by a work situation for a long period of time, it is fair to gently point this out: 'Wow, you've been unhappy with your boss's attitude for the past year, haven't you?'

Listen and ask, don't tell. Just because the whiner doesn't want you to solve everything doesn't mean you should tune out. Listen. That's what she really wants. And ask questions so that she can arrive at her own conclusions, such as, 'Do you want to leave your job?'

Sex in the Workplace

THE CRUSH

You like the new man in marketing. You really like him. He's cute, funny and sexy as hell. You can't help yourself when he's around – you giggle like a high school kid. You have a crush. Problem is, you're married. You're Ms Faithful, so it's not really a problem, but it does whiff of inappropriateness. Married, living with someone or just plain going steady, your work crush may be harmless, but unless you follow certain rules of propriety you may end up sending the wrong signals. The Fabulous Girl can follow this 'crush course' for playing it safe with the guy she can't take her eyes off.

Coming clean

Sure you work together, but if the object of your affection happens to be a newbie, he may not know you're spoken for. He may, in fact, be attracted to you too. You both flirt and enjoy each other's company, so when do you let him know you're married? Before it becomes clear that the flirtations are not so innocent. In other words, before the two of you are groping in the copy room. And tell him yourself. Don't wait for him to ask after you've had après-work drinks. It is best to mention your significant other as soon as you realize you find yourself becoming smitten. This will probably keep both of you in the right headspace.

Affectionate stalking

In other words, putting yourself into your crush's path at every opportunity, hoping for a smile or quick chat to show him how charming and witty you are. It's easy to trick yourself into thinking there's nothing wrong with this kind of behaviour. Sure he seems to notice you too, but being there at his every turn will give him the message that perhaps it's an affair you're after.

Easy on the e-mails

E-mail is dangerous territory for anyone experiencing a crush. Not only will you end up flirting, you will use up half your day doing it. When composing an e-mail to your crush, you will obviously want it to sound cute and cheeky, which is much more time consuming than you think. Not to mention the dangers of being caught sending personal, flirtatious e-mails on company time.

Keep it to yourself

There is something about having a crush that makes us need to talk about the person in his or her absence. Everyone will note if you're constantly talking about Bingo in accounting, but not discussing work – rather, 'Bingo really loved that movie, did you see it?' This is especially true of your spouse. Your husband/boyfriend doesn't need to hear you sing the praises of your crush. If you mention Bingo more than three times in one week, your spouse will probably suspect something and may even ask you if you have a crush, which of course you'll deny. But it's just that Bingo is so brilliant . . . Get real.

Kissing is cheating

All you did was slip him the tongue at the company Christmas party – surely that doesn't count, does it? Yes, it does. A one-two peck on the cheek is one thing; swapping spit is another. You've now taken the crush too far – what you want is an affair. If you really think there is nothing wrong with an 'innocent' kiss, then ask your husband/ boyfriend his opinion.

OOPS, WE KISSED!

If you are single and so is Bob from Accounts, then you may find yourself at an after-work lounge with one glass of champagne too many and Bob's hand up your skirt and your lips on his. If afterwards you realize that (a) Bob is not really the intellect you took him for, (b) he's a lousy kisser or (c) you really like Bill in Accounts, then you may have to end it before it begins.

First of all, don't pretend nothing happened. It did, and both of you know it. No need to be schools kids all over again. No silly notes, awkward glances or silent treatment.

Walk up to Bob and tell him the truth: 'I think things got out of hand last night . . . I'm really not ready to start something.'

Of course, you could find yourself in the situation in which you now love Bob, Bob is everything. But Bob is acting like he doesn't know you. You'll have to be the grown-up and confront him. Do it sooner rather than later. If you let it build up, you'll end up shouting at him in cube country when what you need is privacy. Even a lift will do. It is not rude to ask him what is wrong and why he's being a boor. If he's just going to stammer at you and not give any reasonable form of conversation, then it is clear: you really did make an error of judgment, so move on and e-mail Bill.

GETTING CAUGHT

As a wise FG once said, you can never underestimate the thrill of sex with the boss. However, sex with a non-superior co-worker can also add a bit of sass to your work day. It may be that the Fabulous Girl and Bingo have been at it for months unbeknownst to anyone. With your secret safe, taking greater risks may seem easy as pie – until you're half naked atop the photocopier when your manager strolls in with a stack of contracts. If caught in the buff or partial buffness, the FG can only cover herself and apologize. Tell the manager (who by now has fled the scene in shock) that it will never happen again. And hope that your company does not have a 'no relationships' policy between employees. If it does, see 'You're Fired.'

FG as Her Own Spin Doctor

Inevitably, the Fabulous Girl will find herself having to attend company functions. Say, an awards dinner banquet or company retreat. While it all may seem like a party, getting rip-roaring drunk is not a wise or decorous move. Perhaps the FG is frustrated with her job, or is so stressed she feels the need to let her hair down – regardless, her colleagues are really her colleagues and shouldn't be mistaken for college roommates. In other words, they will judge your behaviour. If, however, you do down six martinis and wind up on the balcony of the five-star hotel tossing a roll of toilet paper onto the street while your entire company watches, you will have some sucking up to do.

If you're very lucky, a close friend you work with will escort you to your room or home, sober you up and be there in the morning to help unravel the mystery in your head. But then it's damage control time. You must learn to be your own spin doctor. Set up a meeting with your boss pronto and tell him or her that you are sorry and make appropriate excuses: stress, family trouble, whatever.

When you face your co-workers for the first time, it is best not to mention the incident unless they do. They may make a joke, in which case you should laugh along then change the subject. If they say nothing, which is really the polite response to another's transgression, then do not bring it up yourself. Unless you personally owe someone an apology, just move along. Something else will occur in the meantime to distract the gossips. But know that your colleagues will tell the tale of your escapades for years, longer than you will probably have the job. This last reason should be enough to follow the simple rule of company functions: do not drink too much.

The Business Trip

If your job involves travel, you must learn to suffer in silence. Everyone around you, and most of all your non-travelling work-mates, will assume the work-related trips are the biggest perk going. And to some degree they are. But they are also a disruption from your life and home comforts, they are tiring and they are work – often more than work done at home office. You are necessarily spending longer hours on the company clock (even if your company does not want to acknowledge this). It's difficult to catch up on what you've missed once you return. But the only people you can really complain to about these hassles are fellow travellers. When you are getting ribbed about your glamorous job, it is best just to smile and say, 'Yes, I'm very lucky.' There's no point in explaining to people why it's hard – they'll never understand.

TIME

If you travel frequently for work, you may want to work out a time travelling/time off arrangement with your firm. A day spent working away from the office almost always involves more hours than a day at the office. Really, the entire time you are away you are on company time. Discuss with your boss the possibility of taking at least a day off (with pay) for every week you are away on business. Preferably, you'd like to take these days as soon as you get back.

THE HOME OFFICE BASE

It's important to lay down some ground rules with the people you work with if you are frequently away on business. First of all, you must insist that they behave as if you are working. Somehow it is difficult for people to believe that although you are in Paris you are not on vacation (however, if you really were on holiday, they would think twice about sending you ten or eleven e-mails a day, wouldn't they?). Ask your assistant, or whoever will be in touch with you most often, to try to call once a day with all the concerns of the day rather than every time something comes up. Also, ask that he or she be sensitive to how information is being translated. If there is nothing you can do about a problem from where you are, it is more disruptive than productive to receive hysterical calls about the situation. And remind people before you leave what the time differences are. You'd think that grown-ups would know that New York is five hours behind London, but sometimes they don't. More than one FG has been woken up in the middle of the night while away on business by a call from the office.

EXPENSE ACCOUNTS

Bless them. A corporate credit card is one of the nicest things in an FG's life. She knows how to use it with respect and care, but she loves it, loves it, loves it. A credit card that someone else pays for – what's not to love? When you're away on business, it pays to be thoughtful about how you handle your expense account. Bring along a bunch of empty envelopes to put each day's receipts into rather than jamming them into your wallet until you get back home. You are not obliged to live like a pauper when you are away for work, but you shouldn't go crazy either. Wine with dinner is fine, but a round of champagne for everyone at the hotel bar is out of the question. Room service for breakfast is nice, but you can probably get a better and cheaper dinner away from the hotel. The key is balance. If you spend little on breakfasts and lunches while you're away, then the dinner that you treat yourself to – and somehow business trips are always in cities where everything is pricier – won't raise any red flags with the accounting department.

Hotel phone bills are always a robbery. However, it doesn't make sense to be self-conscious every time you need to make a call. You *are* working, after all. Also, since you are being separated from your regular life to be at work it is reasonable for you to make calls home on the company bill. One brief call home to your mate or kids each day is well within reason. If you are travelling often, you should consider getting an international mobile phone and billing your company for the calls you make on trips. It will be much cheaper than using the hotel line, and they are usually beautifully designed little things that look chic when whipped out of your handbag.

BOY TOY

There's not much nicer than being able to offer your boyfriend or husband a little trip to New York because you'll be there for business. By all means, ask him along. It doesn't cost your company anything to have your man stay with you. But you do need to be careful about how you handle your expenses if your man joins you. Obviously, your company is not going to pay for his trip as well. And just as obviously, you're not going to stop him from ordering breakfast from the room service menu when you do. Just make sure it comes out even. Go out for dinner or lunch, but don't include that receipt if there are a couple of breakfasts, including two stacks of pancakes. You might also include a note explaining the situation when you submit your receipts.

Make clear to your sweetheart that, although you are thrilled to have him with you, this is primarily a work trip and you need to fulfill your duties before heading out on the town with him. If your love is the adventurous sort, this will not pose a problem. He will happily go off on his own to check out the new exhibition at the Whitney while you are in meetings and then rendezvous with you at the hotel for an afternoon tryst. If your beau is not so independent, it may be better to leave him at home. It's straining to be worried about rushing back to entertain a sulking boyfriend when you need to be focusing on impressing a new client.

WELCOME HOME

As was mentioned before, co-workers will not be entirely sympathetic to your jet lag. However, people should greet you with a 'Hello, welcome back' or 'How was your trip?' before launching into what you forgot to do before you left or what has to be done this very second.

Down and Out

YOU'RE FIRED!

Getting fired is about the worst thing that can happen to an FG – particularly if she is accused of a wrong. If your boss is determined that it was you who stole the missing coffee money and tells you to pack up your desk, there's little that you can do about it at that moment. Take a deep breath, go to the ladies' room if necessary, and pull yourself together. Don't let anyone see you cry. Go to your boss's office and tell her in the calmest possible voice, 'You are making a mistake. I did not steal anything at all. If you don't drop this accuation, you'll be hearing from my lawyer. I'm very sorry our relationship has to end in this way.' And then head out the door.

No matter what you do, the phone lines will be burning up with news of your sacking. This kind of story is simply too juicy for people to do anything other than pick it apart with some amount of glee. This, too, will be a terrible blow to the FG. Even people she has known professionally, people who like and admire her, will be dissecting her fate. More than ever, she must keep her head held high. If you reply to questions with 'It's a very disappointing situation. I'm not able to discuss it, but I'm confident that it will be cleared up soon,' you will give the best impression possible.

Being fired does present another role for the FG spin doctor. When interviewing for new positions, ensure that you do not use the opportunity to rant about how awful your past job was or to cut up your former boss or other colleagues. This is only a poor reflection on you, and it will instantly result in having your name crossed off the short list.

You may not have to broach the subject of your being fired at all. Most prospective employers ask only why you left your last position and will not demand, 'Were you fired?' If your interviewer asks if he can phone your old boss for a recommendation, you are going to have to come a little clean. Explain that unfortunately you and your last employer did not see eye to eye by the end of your job, and that you know that the reference will not be a good one. You can't stop him from calling your old boss, but also offer other references to balance what will certainly be a negative review.

BETWEEN JOBS

Even if you've lost a job through no fault of your own, it is still a devastating experience. Everyone will tell you not to take it personally, but of course you do. It's you. And your job. Well, it *was* your job. How you handle the change in public can determine how quickly you get back on your feet. You don't have to be a big faker, but you should try to stay upbeat, at least when you're describing the situation at a cocktail party. It's a sad fact of life that people don't want to be around misery guts. Better to tell people that it's an unfortunate reality that many law firms are scaling back and that a few people at your company were let go, but that on the up side you're finally able to take that French immersion course you've been wanting to take for the past five years. Also, try to play down the financial duress you are probably under right now. Even if you go home and cry your eyes out, it's better to leave people with the impression that you are a fulfilled and vital person with or without a job. You are also much more likely to attract a new job with this reputation.

FIRING SOMEONE

This is never pleasant, even if you despise the person. You'll be nervous, but you know it must be done. Before firing an employee, be sure to discuss it with the human resources department of your company, or if such a person doesn't exist, a lawyer. Employment laws concerning dismissals are very specific; make sure you've got all your ducks in a row before storming into a potentially litigious situation. Your own boss will know this is happening and will be prepared to back you up if need be. Tell the person the real reasons it is not working out. Keep it brief. Chances are he or she knows what you say is true, but these scenes can get ugly, which is why many companies use security to escort fired employees out of the building.

'Why didn't you tell me?' Finally I was speaking to Eleanor, but I'd had to phone her again. She was still in the suburbs. I didn't know what to tell her. She accused me of keeping the truth about Bingo from her. Had I not been at the Spanks opening? Why didn't I ask Dudley not to write about it?

Eleanor was right, I had been at Spanks. But I had to tell her that I didn't actually see Bingo doing anything with Mel other than talking. As for asking Dudley anything, Eleanor had obvious illusions about my relationship with the wretch.

'I would have warned you, but honestly, I didn't know that anything had happened, let alone that Dudley would write about it.'

Eleanor seemed placated when we hung up, but I couldn't stop thinking about her and Bingo. Not just how awful the entire situation was, but how Dudley had made it so much worse with his rude gossip.

Then I had a thought: why not write about it? I could write an article about the inherent rudeness of gossip. How it was bad manners to make nasty observations and to spread rumours. The piece could distinguish between innocent, fun comments and hurtful, back-stabbing slander. I wanted to write a treatise on how a polite person would handle gossip and being gossiped about. Finally, something to sink my teeth into, something I really cared about that might make a difference. To my friend, anyway.

The next morning I was determined to pitch my manners article, but I had one huge obstacle: big boss Bradley. Before I launched into my pitch, I apologized again for what I'd said about his wife.

'Everyone's entitled to their own opinion,' he said with a grimace.

I realized I was on thin ice suggesting a story about etiquette given my blunder the day before, but I went ahead anyway.

'Manners are boring. No one would want to read *that* stuff,' he spoke into his computer screen.

I gripped my chair. Bradley hated me now, and I guessed that he wouldn't care what I did. I took a chance.

'Can I pitch it to a newspaper?'

He smirked.

'Yeah, go ahead.'

Permission granted, I dialled up the section editor at the paper. But not just any paper. If I was going to write this type of opinion piece, it had to run in *Dudley's* paper. The section editor liked my pitch, especially when I intentionally let it slip that it was inspired by Dudley's gossip column and that in a sense mine was a rebuttal of sorts.

'Can I get it by tomorrow, noon?'

After I hung up the phone I looked at my watch. How could I? But a funny thing happened at my computer. The words flowed, I typed like mad and in only an hour and a half I had an 800-word story. I read it and re-read it. This manners thing came naturally to me. I had always been interested in decorum and in the social skills that could make life smoother – I had once joked that I could write a book about it – but I had never really given it serious thought. Until that moment. I handed in my copy early.

Two days later I pranced into the *Smack!* office with a copy of my article in the paper. It looked fabulous and I loved seeing my name there.

'What's that?' Cheryl asked, a stack of old magazines in her hand.

'My piece I wrote on manners – it's in today's paper.'

'Huh. Oh, that's nice. Now, can you photocopy this stuff for me? I've marked the pages.'

She dropped the stack of mags onto my desk and walked away. That was the other part of my associate editor job, slave labour. I didn't really mind – I just wished that after a year I wouldn't be asked to do that stuff anymore. Feeling chuffed about my article, I decided I would be more grown up at work. I delegated the copying to an intern.

I had to finish writing my usual restaurant roundup for *Smack!*, I watched Bradley come into the office. He had the paper in his hand. I guess I was silly to think he'd be impressed with my work or would somehow value me more as an employee. After all, I had made an ass out of myself at lunch, and why should he forgive me? But that was no excuse for him to be rude, was it? Shouldn't he be gracious and congratulate me?

'I told you to photocopy the pages.' Cheryl towered over me.

'Um, I was busy so I gave it to an intern.'

'Next time, tell me if you can't and I'll find someone else. Really, when I ask you to do something, you should do it.'

So much for my great story and moving up in the world. I settled into my work and later that day prepared for the other facet of my role as associate editor of *Smack!*: social butterfly.

CHAPTER TWO

Society

I had done the party circuit when I had been a freelancer, but when I came on staff, my invitations to parties, launches and events had doubled. Some were boring, but others were pretty fab.

The first big event of the social season had arrived, mere days after the Bingo-as-lout outing in the paper. Missy and I were determined that Eleanor should not hide and we pretty much forced her to attend the party. It was an art opening at one of the city's swankiest galleries and, being an art director at an interior design magazine, she would normally be there – normally on Bingo's arm, but still, she'd be there.

Missy arrived at my place with her car and driver idling outside. This was an added perk for me from Missy's new station in life. I did drive, but having the chauffeur thing was admittedly irresistible: I didn't worry about how much I had to drink, and I didn't need to pay for cabs.

Our priority for the night was simple: Get Bingo. We wanted to ensure that when he laid eyes on Eleanor, he'd regret Mel. Eleanor, for her part, was terrified of seeing him, but she knew she had to get that first brush with him over with. She wasn't ever going to get back with him again, but they hadn't spoken since the Dudley column so she needed us for backup. In order to be fully prepared, we put the finishing touches on Eleanor's Fuck-You Dress, a strapless cocktail number. Tight, yes. Sophisticated, yes. Slutty, no. She looked positively vampy.

'Where's Nice?' Missy always wanted to know where Nice was.

'He should be here any minute.' Nice was my lovely boyfriend. He was all things good: polite, kind, honest and sexy as hell. We'd been together for almost a year and things had been going swimmingly. He was a real grown-up, not one of those dark brooders or super-slick busy guys. He was simply Nice and I loved him.

'Why didn't Joe come tonight?' Eleanor asked.

Missy just shrugged. We didn't push it, but Missy didn't seem too happy.

'Can I join the party?' Nice had arrived. Kitty, my little ginger cat, raced to the door as always, wanting to sink her claws into him before I could.

'I'm so glad you're here.' I kissed him long and hard.

The opening was swarming with people, which wasn't a bad thing as Bingo-and-Mel sightings would be minimal. I was going to keep my eye out for Dudley, which wouldn't be hard – it was never difficult to pick him out of a crowd. He was tall and scrawny, and had a prematurely stoopy posture – very Ichabod Crane – but most remarkable was his near-white blond hair, which he wore perpetually greased back, exposing his abnormally high forehead.

In the meantime, I had another game plan to put into action. I had rehearsed Eleanor and Missy in the art of the snub. Besides arming Eleanor with her Fuck-You Dress, we had vowed not to acknowledge Bingo, Mel or particularly Dudley. You see, neither Eleanor nor I could yell at Dudley or respond to his column in person (and I doubted he'd discuss my manners piece with me). However, we could ignore him en masse, pretend he didn't even exist.

We were simply not going to see him. But in order to maximize the effect, we had to ensure that Dudley saw us not seeing him.

'I'll get us some cocktails,' Nice offered.

'I'll help you.' Missy trotted off beside him.

'I think someone has a crush.'

I didn't respond to Eleanor because ten feet in front of us in the middle of the mix of scruffy painters and slick collectors, were Bingo and Mel, and they were talking with Dudley. I couldn't believe my eyes. It wasn't as though Bingo was telling him off either – they were engaged in what appeared to be a social conversation. There were chortles. There were shoulder slaps. There was friendship.

'I have to go.' Eleanor abandoned me mid-snub. Without them noticing, I too retracted into the crowd. I had to regroup – this social snubbing was trickier than I thought. Eleanor had found Missy and Nice and the four cocktails. Only one drink survived – Eleanor had chugged back three flutes of champagne.

'Here he comes,' warned Missy.

I turned around, trying to be casual. There stood the man, Dudley, rocking back and forth on his brogues, ready to speak. I scanned the room around his twiglike body, never looking directly at him, then turned my back to him as if I hadn't seen him at all. The girls and Nice fell into the act, and we all chatted and laughed. Dudley stalked away. We had succeeded in our plan. But I couldn't help wondering what Dudley had wanted to say. Was he going to apologize to Eleanor? Had he read my article and regretted some of his actions?

I'd never know, for the rest of the evening became a veritable snub-a-thon, with Bingo, Mel and Dudley sightings every five minutes. But my main concern was Eleanor. Knowing how difficult an evening this was, I wanted to

55

distract her. Keeping her out of eye- and earshot was really the best medicine. I took her by the elbow on a tour of the art in the room. It was an unsettling show, with video panels blinking text and images, all revolving around the theme of anxiety. Eleanor was miserable.

'I wonder if Bingo misses me.'

'I think you've had too much to drink,' I offered.

'Maybe you're right, I'm going to the bathroom.' Eleanor trundled off.

Nice came and put his arm around my waist. I leaned into him.

'Do you think that man Dudley will actually care that you're ignoring him? Aren't you making things worse?'

I stopped leaning and turned to face Nice. 'He really hurt my best friend, and I won't stand for it. I'm not going to try and destroy the man, I just want him to know not to mess with us.'

Nice nodded and I hoped he understood. I also hoped my plan would work and that Dudley would leave us alone.

Society

As two wise women once wrote, 'Society is a Fabulous Girl's best friend.' She is both buoyed and shaped by society. She loves meeting new people and is open to new social adventure. Always stylish and civilized, the FG excels in communicating and socializing with everyone she meets in her days and nights. These are the vital players in her life and, in good times, dealing with them is a piece of cake. But no matter how skilled the FG is, there will be situations that will spiral out of her control. Whether she's putting her foot in her mouth or attending a party alone or – worse – involved in a public scandal, she must try to navigate these turbulent moments as if they were well within her command.

Your Reputation

It may sound Victorian but, like it or not, a woman can still carry the social stigma of a bad reputation. She can be known as a 'slut,' 'sponger,' or 'man-poacher.' While such labels are old-fashioned and silly, women still seem ready to hang them on each other, and some even seem to enjoy spreading the bad word. Of course one can have a good reputation too. In any case, the very notion of a woman's reputation as something that is decided not only by her but also by the society she moves in still packs a wallop. Nonetheless, the reality is that a woman can achieve any reputation she wants, and on occasion there may even be advantages to cultivating a bad one.

GET THE REPUTATION YOU WANT

The Fabulous Girl wants her friends and colleagues to think of her as, well, fabulous. To ensure this opinion she needs to act the part. The Fabulous Girl is someone who is an integral part of her social set. She puts herself out there socially by attending parties, art openings and other events. She plays host too. The FG is someone who values style and considers it part of her contribution to society. Included in her definition of style is an interest in the arts, literature, politics and whomever she is conversing with. And, of course, she must be polite.

One thing that makes the FG stand out is her confidence. She does not indulge her shyness; she shares her opinions. She even talks about her commitment to good manners, for instance. Of course, we don't mean she should talk incessantly about herself or lecture others on how to behave, but certainly action speaks louder than words. So behave like an FG, and you will be one.

SALVAGE THE ONE YOU HAD

No amount of pre-emptive fabulousness can protect the FG in every crisis. If you had the reputation of being a nice, loyal friend but ended up stealing your best friend's husband, then understandably your reputation has been altered. How does an FG find herself in such a mess? She doesn't wake up one morning and decide, 'Today I'm going to destroy my friend's marriage.' She is not a man-poacher by design. Perhaps the man in question is in a very unhappy relationship, a fact confirmed for the FG by his wife. People fall in love with the wrong people all the time. The Fabulous Girl may find herself caught between her heart and her friendship. Naturally this affair is not fabulous, but as a wise FG once said, 'Life gets messy and complicated, but how you handle the mess can make or break your reputation (not to mention your sense of self).'

However, even the most damaged reputation can be salvaged – if on such a downslide you behave with grace. In this instance, the FG wouldn't gloat about her new boy prize or defend herself to people by cutting up her old friend, no matter how the wounded friend may verbally attack her.

In any such extreme situation, apologize to the friend or whomever your actions hurt, taking full responsibility for your bad deed. Then keep a low profile until the dust settles. Inevitably, people will move on and turn their attention to fresher gossip. It may also be time to work on new friendships while keeping your distance from the old group.

ALTER THE ONE YOU'VE GOT

But what of our FG who wants to dabble? She's always been good – maybe too good. She frets that men find her too nice to seduce and her employer thinks her too meek to manage. Well, the solution is in the presentation.

With lovers or potential lovers, you may want to be more daring, in your dress and in your demeanour. When out socially, you may flirt a little more outrageously, wear something a bit more sexy. Maybe you'll invite him out for an after-party cocktail or make the first move on the guy who refuses to think of you in that way.

At work put more polish into your delivery. You can start this by crisping up your wardrobe. In most work environments, people associate a pulled-together, even slightly formal wardrobe with seniority. Work this angle. More important, though, is your demeanour. Start speaking up at meetings, offering your thoughts and suggestions to discussions. If you've been a quiet member of the team, you will definitely get noticed if you raise your voice. Find ways to spend time with important people in your office and in your field. When you're at a work event, don't be too shy to go up to the people you admire and simply introduce yourself to begin with. Compliment them on a project they worked on recently. The next time you see them, you'll more easily fall into conversation and make an impression. These are the kinds of relationships you should build on – they allow you to get the word out in your industry that you want to be taken seriously.

Likewise, if you have a reputation as a coke-head party girl and you want to play straight, be honest and tell people that you've cleaned up your act and are focusing on your career now (or art or whatever). Dump your friends from the party world and cultivate acquaintances with the people you wish to emulate. Change your manner, your wardrobe, your way of talking and your bedtime. Be seen leaving the bar at 11 P.M. and not after it closes. You may be regarded with suspicion or even ridicule at first, but time will prove the deciding factor on your reputation makeover.

A technique for changing one's reputation is to switch social circles. Creating a different image is easier if you're not surrounded by those who will only ever see you as your old self. This is not to say that you must cut everyone from your life, just expand your list of acquaintances and spend time with different sorts who won't question why you're suddenly discussing poetry so much. Then, as your confidence builds, even the old friends will come around and embrace the change.

The Fabulous Girl must realize that her reputation cannot be made in one day, week or month. And all of these alterations to her behaviour must be parcelled out gradually so that she eases into her new attitude. They must also be repetitive or else it won't be a new reputation but a mere blip in her love life or career.

The Art of Conversation

It is an often-neglected art these days, but for the Fabulous Girl being a good conversationalist is a top priority. She needs to converse with people from all walks of life, from the plumber to the banker, with the same attention and politeness. Why? People will remember the FG who listens well and who treats them with respect. She knows life runs better if you take the time to make conversation with all of the people in it. The banker will return her calls, the mechanic will fix her car while she waits and the editor will give her the story assignment. Also, the Fabulous Girl will learn more about people, how the world works and valuable facts and tips that may come in handy later (including as conversation starters). This may sound simplistic or clichéd but as anyone who has been party to bad small talk can attest, the ability to strike up a conversation is not always a natural character trait. But it can be learned. It should be simple: you talk for a bit, then I talk for a bit, I ask you a question and wait for a reply, I show some interest in that reply, you reciprocate with some curiosity of your own.

Instead, what passes for conversation in many sophisticated circles is more like a battle for air time: I sit through your noises until you need to inhale, then I jump in and make noise until you cut me off to make some more of your own. All this 'me' and 'no, me' just doesn't cut it in polite company. The FG has studied and perfected her own set of rules for giving great gab:

1. Listen. Don't just wait for your conversational partner to stop talking. By all means, add your thoughts to whatever it is they're saying. It's all too clear when people aren't listening, though. Bingo is regaling a group at a cocktail party about his trip to surf school in Hawaii and Jessica jumps in

and says, 'Oh, that reminds me of the time I lived in Guam for the winter.' If this is your conversational tactic, you can be sure everyone is thinking, 'Huh?'

2. Be aware of whom you are talking to. Does everyone in the conversational circle know about medieval pig farming? You don't have to avoid your favourite topic if the entire group is not up to speed on it, but you do have to be sure to fill them in. Of course, if you find yourself in the middle of a topic you don't know anything about, it's your job to pipe up and ask questions rather than sit there getting irritated. Likewise, beware of shop talk in mixed company. Sticking for long stretches of time to conversational topics that necessarily exclude some people at a party is simply rude.

3. Ask questions. Nothing is more tedious than people whose idea of conversation is to outline their latest accomplishments. There's nothing wrong with filling people in on what you've been up to or sharing a piece of good news, but be sure to take a real interest in the other person as well.

FOOT-IN-MOUTH DISEASE

Everyone is capable of saying the wrong thing at the wrong time. The Fabulous Girl is no exception. You opine to your acquaintance, Bob, during a work event that you find the latest soft drink ad campaign to be insipid and lacking in imagination. Later that evening, another colleague tells you that Bob was the creative force behind that very soft drink ad. The realization that you've put your foot in your mouth is alarming. You secretly wish Bob had offered up the truth before you continued your critical tirade and made such an ass of yourself. But then you understand that Bob was trying to be polite. What to do? Damage control, of course. You must immediately find Bob and have a chuckle over your indiscretion. Apologize and explain that clearly you had no idea of the connection, but be light-hearted, even admitting what a dummy you are. Bob may not feel better, but he will accept your apology. Though Bob may now be plagued by self-doubt, but hey, who isn't sometimes?

If you find yourself on the other side of Foot-In-Mouth Disease, then it's most polite to let the ranter in on misunderstanding as soon as possible. However, you must be able to make the person feel better about the mistake, so you can't then take the ranter to task for poor taste in soda commercials. You may think it's better to behave as Bob did and just keep quiet, but inevitably people will realize they've put their foot in it and feel like idiots – better to just get it over with.

If you notice a friend putting her foot in it, as discreetly as possible take her aside and fill her in on her gaffe.

THE WALLFLOWER FACTOR

If you are the shy, silent type, chances are you tremble in fear as you approach the door of the event or party you know you must attend. Your fear only increases when you enter and realize that, exactly as you thought, you don't know anyone, or at best you've had vague introductions to people who may or may not remember you. This is surely one of the most challenging situations for the Fabulous Girl as she moves through life.

But shyness is not an excuse for avoiding social situations. Rest assured that no one enjoys standing alone in a crowd feeling like the only stranger in the room. So take a deep breath and a sip of champagne, and introduce yourself. Make an effort by asking people about themselves and you may develop the reputation of being an excellent listener. Of course, you also run the risk of never getting a word in, but you can't have it both ways. If you do connect well with someone new, make sure that you do not monopolize him for the entire evening. Your new pal may find you fascinating but he may also be eager to chat with others in the room. If you sense his interest is waning it's time to make a break.

It may sound silly, but a trip to the ladies' room can be good for shy girls on two counts. First, it gets you out of the room for a few minutes and allows you to pull yourself together if you're feeling uncomfortable. But the other bonus is the mysterious atmosphere of a women's washroom, which allows perfect strangers to strike up conversation with each other. Ask the woman at the next sink for the time, and pretty soon you're chatting away.

It is also wise to give yourself a time limit. If you decide ahead of time that you're going to give the party 45 minutes, then do so. Parties shouldn't be a chore. And when you've been at the party for 45 minutes, had a couple of drinks, made a few conversations and you've had enough, then head home with your head held high.

If you are the one speaking with a shy person, at least make one or two attempts at conversation. But if the person still won't say boo, it's time to move on.

COCKTAIL OPENERS

Banter. Chat. Repartee. Whatever you call it, witty and appropriate conversation at a cocktail party can make or break an FG's rank on the invite lists of many hosts. For example, on one occasion an FG invited a new acquaintance to a particularly swank party at an artist's loft in Hoxton. A group of guests had been casually discussing the best boutiques in Notting Hill when the new girl interjected with, 'My boyfriend has a ten-inch cock.' Everyone was stunned into silence. There's nothing wrong with making a provocative remark to rev up a dull conversation, but an FG stays within the limits of polite society.

However, even the Fabulous Girl can get rusty between social seasons. Fortunately, there are a few opening lines that never fail and aren't the least bit tacky. Remember, it is your job as a guest, be it at a house party or a charity ball, to be polite, friendly and charming.

Introduce yourself

As soon as you realize you are standing next to someone you don't know, stick out your hand and say hello. This is particularly important if you're with people who are bad with names and therefore with introductions.

'How do you know Bingo?'

The easiest way to strike up a conversation with a stranger is to ask her about her relationship with the host or the guest of honour.

'I love your dress.'

Shoes. Eyewear. Whatever. You can never go wrong opening a cocktail conversation with a piece of flattery. As long as you're sincere, there's nothing more socially lubricating. And it's nearly impossible not to find something praiseworthy.

'You had me at hello.'

One of the most challenging conversation hurdles is what to say to the handsome man you're dying to meet. If you're lucky, a friend or colleague will supply the introduction. If not, keep it simple and try a smile, your name and, sure, go for the above-mentioned compliment. But don't blurt out, 'You're the sexiest man in the room,' even if you think he is.

'Can I get you another drink?'

If you have nothing to say, a trip to the bar just might be the pause that refreshes. Come back with a few observations to share along with those martinis. And yes, all you Fabulous Girls out there, this means you. There's something just plain chic about offering to get a guy a drink (okay, beer not so much), and men appreciate that independent forties-film-star type. Lauren Bacall was forever fixing cocktails for Bogie!

'I'm between books – have you read a good one lately?'
A multiple-tangent topic. If he says he never has time to read, ask him how he does like spending his free time.

'How is work?'
While the first question out of your mouth should never be 'What do you do for a living?' the old rule about avoiding shop talk during the cocktail hour just doesn't apply anymore. People spend hours and hours at their jobs, and they are far more likely to have something interesting to say about their work than about their non-existent hobbies. Be open-minded; while selling insurance may be a deadly dull topic, your new friend may have hidden talents and interests.

'How about that slide show?'
If you're trying to engage a stranger in conversation, it can be wise to comment on the evening's festivities, be it the silent auction items or the soprano who just wouldn't shut up about her latest CD before singing her aria.

'I haven't heard this music before – do you know what it is?'
It doesn't really matter what the answer is. It's a gateway topic.

'Be seasonal.'
Get a little more adventurous than 'Terrible weather isn't it?'
In spring try, 'Are you a gardener?' In summer ask, 'Any
holiday plans?' to get the conversation started.

FG TO THE RESCUE

Just because the rudeness wasn't directed at her doesn't
mean an FG can watch silently while others are insulted.
When she sees someone being treated badly, an FG
commiserates with the victim. At the very least she makes eye
contact with the person who has been treated rudely and
shakes her head in sympathy. But a true FG sticks up for the
underdog. Politely, of course. If you notice a pregnant
woman or an elderly person standing on the bus – and you
are standing yourself, of course – you can pleasantly ask
someone to give up her seat. Very often people just aren't
thinking and need only a little nudge to do the right thing.
However, if the situation is more extreme, an FG ups the
ante. If you witness a co-worker being unreasonably snappish
or condescending to his or her assistant, speak up: 'Wow, you
were really harsh with Linda there. If you've got a problem
with her, maybe you should talk it over with her.'

Jealousy

You're still struggling in your Jill job but your best friend has
suddenly landed her dream position. The ex-boyfriend who
broke your heart has finally gotten his big break in show
business. Sure, you're happy for him, right? Right? Admit it,
this type of situation can make even the most stable FG recoil
just a bit. 'Why not me?' she may ask herself. And let's be
honest, if the super-successful person happens to be someone

you don't like, or whom you even despise, you're certainly not going to be happy for him. You're going to be rancid. You can't believe that Plum got that weekly travel spot on your fave daily TV news show, and now she'll be jet-setting around the globe for free and you have to see her stupid face on the tube and hear how fab she is when really you know she hasn't an original idea in her head. Yadda yadda yadda. Fine. Don't be happy for her. And let's face it, you're probably right and your opinion is no doubt shared by others you do respect. However, this is where you must up the fabulousness quotient and employ the 'nicing' tactic, where you counter bad behaviour or your own bad feelings with sweetness. You must congratulate Plum, saving your critical musings for your closest friends. Nicing is very useful when you encounter someone in your social circle whom you are irrationally irritated by. You don't want anyone to see you behaving in a jealous manner, and sometimes you can even trick yourself into a more generous attitude this way.

When is it appropriate to criticize? It is not the intention of this book to brush aside all negative opinions or to hide all feelings that aren't 'nice.' But what an FG needs to do is make the distinction between bitchy banter and intellectual debate or constructive criticism. Back to Plum the travel princess. Maybe the FG has a point. What if Plum TV spots are trivial drivel? An FG can extol her opinions in mixed company, and by that we mean the fans and non-fans of Plum. But she needs to do it in a non-snarky way. And she must hear out those who may retort, 'I love Plum, she makes me laugh . . .'

SOCIETY

How to Spot a Social Climber
Without Suspecting Everyone

There's a difference between wanting to meet interesting and successful people and being an obvious social climber. Many hostesses gain reputations for bringing together fab people, some of whom they may not know well at all themselves. This is not social climbing. Of course, there is also nothing wrong with wanting to better your position in society and to have new and interesting people as your friends. But you must cultivate them with subtlety and sincerity, not because you just want to be able to say you know them. Here's how to spot an SC and therefore not become one:

1. They name-drop. Literally. Climbers tend to use and say names more than normal people. They repeatedly mention the name of the musician they were seated next to at a dinner party as if the sound of that person's name uttered over and over somehow suggests a friendship. 'And then Yo-Yo Ma said the funniest thing about wanting some more bread. Yo-Yo Ma really likes bread.'

2. It's in the eyes. Social climbers are hungry, and it always shows in their big, wide eyes.

3. They're rude. SCs tend to look over your shoulder while in conversation – unless you're famous, that is – on the look-out for more desirable prey.

4. They're bold. SCs always ask to be introduced to the highest-status person in the room.

5. They ditch their old friends for bigger and better invites from the bigger and better people, and they won't ask their old friends along.

Fabulous Girl as Bad Girl

SURVIVING A SCANDAL

However much style, grace, intellect and wit she may have, the FG is still human and can make poor judgment calls. Or she may fail to consider the consequences before acting. Sometimes it's an affair of the heart, and in that particular scenario no amount of common sense will dissuade her. For in love, as in art, one can justify almost anything. Being a passionate person, the FG may find herself voicing unpopular opinions that will put her in conflict with powerful people. However it happens, even an FG can find herself in the midst of a scandal.

The upside of being involved in a scandal, however small, is that in certain social circles you may be seen as an even more desirable guest. In this century, a person's cachet may rise out of her involvement in varied sorts of intrigue. 'Good society' has been replaced with 'celebrity society.' People are always interested in innuendo and gossip and want to be on the inside track. Hoping that you may confess your 'sins' or at least tell your side of it is very enticing to many a dinner-party host. Pick your invitations carefully and make sure, if need be, your legal council approves before the RSVP goes out.

The scandalized Fabulous Girl does not, however, spill her guts to this select group. On the contrary, she maintains her composure if prodded, politely changing the subject. The host should ensure that the conversation does not remain on the scandal. In other words, the elephant in the room should be ignored. The 'fallen' FG may add spice to the table, but she is not there to be flambéed.

However, if you're not the one who's been scandalized but a friend or acquaintance of one, then you may need to give some thought to social interactions with that person. If you do want to entertain your friend who is under investigation for insider trading or who left her boyfriend for her boss, you may still do so, but you should keep it simple. A dinner party for ten is fine; a cocktail party for fifty is too much attention for your buddy.

How to snub and survive a snubbing

In the last decades, as social constraints have loosened, people have become increasingly reluctant to judge the character of others. The FG urges a reconsideration of this issue. Think of society as a big sandbox. Those who play nicely may stay, but those who kick sand in the eyes of the other kids must find their own playground. You must, of course, kick people out of the sandbox decorously. Herewith is the FG guide to snubbing and being snubbed.

1. Keep it quiet. Snubbing simply means that you behave as if the offender doesn't exist. It does not involve publicly haranguing or in any way drawing attention to the act of snubbing. You just don't see the offender.

2. Choose your snubbing moments carefully. Snubbing is an extreme social move and must be reserved for extreme situations. The offender must have wronged you in a serious way for snubbing to be considered. If a colleague ate the lunch you put in the office fridge, you might be cross but it is not grounds for the silent treatment. If an acquaintance spreads slanderous rumours about you (restraining orders, an affair with the babysitter) among your social set, snubbing may certainly be in order. A call to your lawyer may also be called for, but at a minimum, snub.

3. Apply pre-emptive snubbing. In most cases, the FG will give all humanity the benefit of the doubt and avoid pre-judging people. There are certain characters in society,

however, who it is reasonable to assume will do you harm – gossip columnists, for instance. These types should not be welcome in polite company. Never assume that they won't use their friendship with you to do their terrible job or get you to say or do something compromising for use as a weapon later. They always do.

4. You may snub only those who have done you, or those extremely close to you, harm. Just because you heard a rumour that Bingo had an affair with his friend's wife five years ago, you may not snub him. It is not your business and you have no snubbing rights.

5. If you are being snubbed you probably know why. You will recall that, in fact, you did have an affair with your friend's boyfriend, and that's why she looks right through you at social functions. If you are being snubbed and don't know why, go ahead and approach the snubber. But don't try to get to the bottom of it at the party where you risk a scene. Call him the next day and ask if you've slighted him without realizing it.

6. If you are the object of a snub and you know why, you may try to get back in favour by apologizing to the appropriate party. If, however, what you did was so horrid that an apology won't suffice, you may have to suffer the consequences of your actions. If you are snubbing someone and she apologizes, you must accept her apology, so ending the snub. While you don't have to be best friends again, you must acknowledge her in public.

Fabulous Girl Private Moments
(OR WHAT *SHOULD* BE PRIVATE)

PUBLIC PREENING – WHERE AND WHEN YOU CAN PRIMP

It is never fabulous to apply a full face of makeup on the train or at your desk (if you work in an open-plan office). While driving, it is both un-fabulous (we can see you) and dangerous (mascara wand through the eyeball, anyone?) to apply makeup. There's something intimate about the act – all that touching of your face – that is simply not appropriate for public viewing. No one is so busy that they can't do this part of their routine at home.

This goes double for anything at all to do with hair. Do not brush your hair in a meeting. Do not brush your hair while you're queuing at the supermarket. Do not brush your hair anywhere in public except the ladies'.

PUBLIC BATHROOMS

This is a subject that the Fabulous Girl would rather not discuss at all. However, it is an area of life that every FG must navigate.

Togetherness

If you and a girlfriend skip to the loo together, it's polite to let conversation fade as you enter the stalls. Many people do not feel comfortable chatting while they use the facilities. Likewise, if you walk into your office's washroom and think you recognize a pal's shoes under the stall door, don't call over. And if you do notice that someone is lingering in a stall, allow her privacy and leave as soon as possible.

Sharing

If the person next to you does pipe up with her need for toilet paper, you must oblige if you can. Polite FGs do not reply that they 'can't spare a square.' And pass over more than you think your neighbour needs.

Keep it neat

While in the stall, please ensure that the toilet is flushed completely and successfully. And remember to wipe the seat before you exit.

Move over

At the sink, if you splash a gallon of water on the counter, take a few seconds to wipe up your mess. And while it is a part of women's culture to preen, make room for those who need the sinks while you are applying your lipstick. It's impolite to block them just because you were there first.

Sex

While it sounds like the stuff of rock-star legend, sex in a public washroom does happen. If you really can't wait until you get home, then at least try to have *polite* tawdry sex. If there are only two stalls and one is broken, use the broken one. Don't get down in the only working stall, leaving a line of crossed-legged women (including a Fabulous Girl one night at a very chic restaurant).

Comfort levels

Just because your last boyfriend had an open-door-while-peeing policy, it does not mean your new sweetheart will be open to it. Always assume that people want complete privacy in the washroom. That includes talking through the door when they are in there. Even peeing in front of other FGs may not go down well.

Fab girl exception

Despite the above rules of decorum, there are certain circumstances where talking is vital, say in the restrooms of nightclubs, bars and restaurants. The bathroom, Ladies', toilet, loo – whatever you wish to call it – is the only place where secrets can be whispered or admissions made during a group outing. Many a decision has been made during lipstick application in the Ladies'. What better time to tell your best pal that Bingo is eyeing her? Or to ask what you should do about Ivan, who can't keep his hands to himself? Or that you want to ditch Ben and go home? Use this time for these little issues and to basically assess the evening. Consider these moments the FG half-time show.

Public peeing

A Fabulous Girl would, of course, never stoop to relieving herself in public no matter how small her bladder is. Answering nature's call outside of nature (that is, camping) is totally inappropriate. Okay, it's gross. Obviously, men are far more guilty of this than women. Men's peeing in public has become such an issue in Europe that monuments – doing double duty as urinals – are actually eroding. Yuk. An FG will strongly discourage any man in her life or her vicinity from behaving in this manner. (Likewise spitting.)

The men's room

You've got to go. Really, really badly. But the Ladies' is being used. Then you spot it, the oasis: a single toilet for men. First you must knock loudly before opening the door to the opposite gender's bathroom, then open the door a crack and announce your intentions of entering. Great, no one is inside. Just be ready for that sinking feeling when someone from the outside tries to get in. A man. You're going to have to face him. Hopefully, he will be a gentleman and smile and say hello – not as has happened, swear and stomp and be all indignant (he who pees in public). If you are treated rudely by the unruly male, just ignore him and go back to your table. He's utterly wrong to berate you for this.

The Party

DRESSING FOR IMPORTANT MOMENTS

An FG understands that her fashion choices can set the tone for just about any moment in her life. Style speaks volumes for her. Sometimes it says the thing she's too much of a lady to say herself.

The Fuck-Me Dress

You're going out on the third date and you're pretty sure that tonight's the night. You don't need to be over-the-top sexy, but you should reach for a Fuck-Me Dress. Which doesn't necessarily have to be a dress at all. Depending on where you're off to, it could be a cashmere top and a pair of jeans that make your bum look fantastic, or a wrap dress that keeps you fairly covered but makes ladies look great. The Fuck-Me Dress doesn't need to show a lot of skin. It's more about the fabric: this is a dress that should make you seem touchable.

The Fuck-You Dress

If you know that your ex is going to be at a party, you're obviously going to pay a little extra attention to your outfit. Whether you go for that outfit he always loved on you or something brand new (really, the better way to go since it implies that your fabulous new life is full of fabulous new things), what you're looking for is a Fuck-You Dress. Go tight, short or low-cut – but only one, whichever works best on you. You want to look sexy without looking slutty.

The Fuck-Her Dress

If the ex is going to be at a party or event with a new girl-friend or perhaps a woman that you have other competitive issues with will be there, the FG has two choices: the Fuck-You Dress or the Fuck-Her Dress. FGs aren't catty by nature, but there are times when a girl needs a little extra armour to get her through the night. However, use restraint as you would when consuming alcohol at such an occasion: avoid that micro-mini, cleavage-to-*there* dress that will only make you appear insecure. Remember, your outfit for feeling good and confident when in the company of this potentially troublesome new girl or definitely troublesome old nemesis should be sexy in a simple, chic and sophisticated way. And remember, women notice details that men never do. Designer duds or fab knock-offs will get her goat, and if the dress itself is simple then jazzing it up with a killer bag, a great pair of shoes or a piece of antique jewellery will give the effect you're looking for.

An FG takes pride in her appearance. She loves clothes and keeps up with fashion and beauty trends. But she knows when to pull back. While dressing, the FG keeps in mind as a cautionary tale the girl who goes too far. The girl who goes too far wears the peasant blouse with the flounced skirt, the rustic sandals and the turquoise jewellery, and carries a straw bag. All at once. This lack of restraint – the overly styled girl in the head to toe Dolce & Gabbana – is Z-list territory. Don't go there.

COCKTAIL-PARTY MISHAPS

There you are, having a lovely time at the cocktail party thrown by Mrs and Mr Fancy. Candles are floating in their backyard pool, the champagne is flowing, the conversation is flirtatious, the dog is peeing on your Prada sandals. Yep. Their beloved dog Rover has escaped from his kennel, made a beeline for you and your most expensive shoes and gone ahead and relieved himself on your left foot. These are the kind of moments which truly test an FG's mettle in the decorum department. You love your Pradas, and even though you love animals you feel like hoofing Rover in the drink. At a minimum you'd like to screech and tear off the now-damp shoes. Alas, as a well-mannered woman you can do neither, particularly if your hosts have witnessed Rover's breach of etiquette. You need to act as if this is the most amusing thing that has ever happened to you. They will naturally feel terrible about it and your job is to make them feel better. Walk over to the pool laughing and say you just must know what the water is like; dunk your whole pee-soaked foot in the pool, give it a shake and ask for another glass of champagne.

If you're the host and such a mishap occurs – say, your guest steps in Rover's 'present' – then you must clean off his shoes. Don't just hand him a paper towel, offer to do it for him. If he refuses and wants to do it himself let him, but by all means take him to another spot, away from the party. There is nothing sexy about watching a person clean dog shit off his sole.

BLURRY NIGHTS

Every once in a while – or for some, every night – we need to go out on the town and let loose. One, two or five cocktails and a bottle of wine later, however, and you may end up saying or doing things you don't really want others to hear or see. For instance, an FG attends a birthday party wearing a striking pair of lace-up stilettos. She drinks a lot. A whole lot. She is barely able to stand up on her high heels. It's time to give the birthday toast. The FG grabs the unopened bottle of champagne, insisting on opening it. The other guests watch nervously as the FG sways, her laces loosening. Just as the cork is about to pop, her laces give way and she falls over, sending the cork flying in the direction of the hosts' plasma television, cracking the screen. You can't help wondering if the next morning she'll be able to face facts let alone the replacement bill for the TV. Of course, it is best not to get so drunk that you do things you later regret, but hey, who are we kidding?

Therefore, in honour of all drunken blurs, the FG has a set of rules for coping with those harrowing realizations on the morning after:

1. The Backtrack. Okay, so you just confessed to your long-term pal your ardent love for him, but it was not reciprocated. Or you invited someone you actually despise to your upcoming dinner party. In situations like these, there is one fortunate fact: the person in question probably has as hazy a memory of the event as you do. In fact, if you were to pretend it never happened, he or she might actually be relieved. But an apology needs to be extended for the blurted words of love that made your friend uncomfortable. Let him or her decide whether to discuss the matter further. The same applies if you have shared too many personal details about yourself or someone else while tipsy. Be honest and ask the recipient to keep it to herself. As for the regrettable invitation to your dinner party – if you cannot cancel then you do have to live with it. You can always make it a big dinner party, or even a buffet style dinner, so you don't have to spend much face time. And who knows, maybe you'll find something to like about the person by the end of it.

2. The Blind Eye. Even if you haven't committed a drunken indiscretion, you might find yourself a witness to one. When you see someone do something you know is embarrassing, it's best to laugh and forget about it.

3. Passes. The most common blunders made while people are under the influence are of a sexual nature. Maybe you've had your eye on that handsome theatre producer for a long

time, or maybe you've just caught sight of that swivel-hipped young architecture student. But suddenly you're locked in an embrace. The next time you see him or her, you must acknowledge that some intimacy has passed between you. Just a note saying 'Oops, we kissed. Thanks' is fine. But if you suspect that your drunken attentions were unwanted, you must certainly apologize. And if you've made such a pass yourself and you are not single, then it may be time to investigate your options.

4. The Repeat Offender. As mentioned, these situations can happen to the most polished FG. But if you repeatedly get so blitzed at parties that you end up doing it in the bathroom with strangers, you've got a big problem, and something stronger than an FG's good advice is called for.

THE FABULOUS-GIRL HANGOVER

Be it during a long night or a long weekend, more than a few FGs have indulged enough to wake up the next morning to a searing headache (especially if all that alcohol was accompanied by a few cigarettes), a reeling stomach and the occasional spinning room. Such experiences will motivate many women to proclaim, 'Never again.' And some may even mean it. But as long as there are hangovers, there will be etiquette issues involved.

1. Take your medicine. Remember, this is a self-inflicted illness, so you really can expect only so much sympathy. Your hangover is no excuse to cancel brunch plans or business meetings. You must graciously crawl to whichever event you are committed to. This, of course, underlines the fact that in accepting invitations or setting up meetings, you are obliged to avoid overindulging the night before.

2. Put a cork in it. Again, you did this to yourself, so cut

out the whining. If you can't stop, then at least sequester yourself in a dark room until it passes.

3. Offer spousal support. While no one enjoys being around a hungover partner, if you are the clean and sober half of the couple (or a flat mate) you must not sneak into the bedroom and whip open the blinds. You will not snap the victim out of her misery. Likewise, this is not the time for lectures, especially in a loud voice. Wait until the next day to broach the subject of overindulgence.

4. Turn over a new leaf. It's not unusual after a few weeks or years of heavy partying for the thought of detoxifying the system to enter some people's minds. With this choice come other measures, such as special diets. If it's a weekend juice fast, it's fairly simple to self-cleanse in private. But if you're after a longer-term diet-and-drink overhaul, you must warn your dinner companions in advance. Though many will do their best to accommodate you, don't expect that heavy drinkers will necessarily want to accompany you to a juice bar.

Fabulous Girl Hot Tip

The Bloody Mary is the best 'hair of the dog' to sooth the savage hangover. To make this delicious cocktail (which is yummy at any hour), fill a highball with ice, and 1¼ fluid ounces of vodka, top with tomato juice and season with Tabasco and worcestershire sauces, with a lime wedge on the edge. If you're not too bleary-eyed, you can first rim the glass with seasoning salt (very tasty).

Fabulous Girl on the Lam

Just as the FG doesn't plan to fall in love with a married man, she also doesn't aspire to be Bonnie Barrow, of Bonnie and

Clyde fame, and lead a life of crime. However, without thinking, she may inadvertently end up on the wrong side of the law. This is a different kind of bad behaviour, beyond the social scandals and love triangles.

DRINKING AND DRIVING

So you have one too many martinis, but you still feel fine. You think you are safe to drive. But you are over the legal limit, and no one else at the party seems to realize it. You leave and get behind the wheel. You take it slow. Too slow. A marauding truck driver spots your tortoise-like speed and calls the cops. Next thing you know, a policeman has blue-lighted you to the shoulder of the highway and you're standing there in your halter gown and strappy stilettos blowing into the Breathalyzer. At least you're trying to. You fail the test like your German GCSE exam, and he plays by the book, snapping the handcuffs on and shoving you into the back seat of the cruiser. Now what?

This is one situation where being fabulous fails, try as you might to behave with grace. You inquire after the cop's family as he fingerprints you. Rather than being charmed, he writes in his report that your chatter indicates you're not taking the charge seriously. You are now a criminal. The FG in such an extreme circumstance will be scared, but she must not throw a diva fit, crying and screaming to be set free. She must be co-operative and polite. She must also call her lawyer and promise to never drink and drive again.

If a Fabulous Girl spots someone unfit to drive, she should speak up. It is not rude to tell a stranger that he or she should call a cab. Or the FG could point out to the host that a guest is too drunk to get behind the wheel.

However, if the FG is called to bail out a friend who has committed such an offence, she shouldn't lecture. The friend no doubt understands the seriousness of the crime and will thank the FG for picking her up from jail.

The FG will not tell all her friends about buddy's adventures or that she lost her licence.

GETTING CAUGHT SHOPLIFTING
(OR AT THE VERY LEAST CAUGHT BY STORE SECURITY)

There is nothing fabulous about stealing (well, maybe if you play an art or jewel thief in a 1950s film set in Europe), yet there are known FG thieves. One very famous FG film star was caught red-handed in a Beverly Hills boutique. She didn't need to steal, she was rich. Sometimes it's simply the thrill of it. If you do get nabbed by those nasty-looking plain-clothes security guys or gals, then you'll have to turn on the charm to prevent them from giving you what you deserve – a trip to the police station. The standard excuse of 'I just dropped it in my handbag to make it easier to carry, then I forgot it was there' may work the first time. But seriously, this type of behaviour or mistake is only barely acceptable for teens in a rebellious phase. If you find yourself drawn to this kind of perilous hijinks, it is something you must discuss with a therapist.

YOUR SHOPLIFTING FRIEND

The store is packed with weekend shoppers, and the teenaged staff can't handle the volume of merchandise and customers coming in and out of the changing room. You and your buddy share a dressing room. Nothing fits so you're ready to take off, when buddy notices that a skirt doesn't have a security tag. A skirt she likes. A skirt that fits her perfectly. She stuffs it into her purse and makes a break for it. Unfortunately, if you find yourself an unwitting accomplice to a shoplifter, there is little you can do outside of scolding your friend. It is not very friendly to turn her in. However, you should nag her about it, even letting it slip while in the company of other friends. This should embarrass her enough to not repeat the offence.

The party had thinned out. A group of artists and writers were going down the street for a punk rock karaoke night. So not our thing. Missy, Nice and I were ready to go home. But Eleanor was still missing in action. It had been twenty minutes since her trip to the bathroom. I volunteered to go find her while Nice and Missy got our coats.

As I passed the bar, I was sideswiped by a tall guy carrying two pints of beer. It was Bingo, too close to ignore.

'Hey, how ya doing?'

'Fine, Bingo. I read about you in the paper.'

'Oh, that. Well, ya know, word gets out. Say, how's Eleanor?'

'How do you think she is?'

He shrugged. Then, unbelievably, he slowly ran his eyes up and down my body.

'You look foxy tonight. Still with that guy?'

'Yes, *that guy* is waiting for me.'

I stormed away. What a bastard. Not only did he have the gall to ask about Eleanor, but he checked me out as if I was auditioning for a live sex show. Yuck.

Enraged, I threw open the ladies' room door. It was empty. But I could hear a woman giggle, a woman who sounded just like Eleanor.

'Eleanor?' I wandered down the line of cubicles, but she

wasn't there. Still the Eleanor-sounding woman was some-where. She seemed to be on the other side of the wall. The men's room. Worried, I raced over, knocked first, then swung open the door. Lucky for me the urinals were unoccupied. But two of the stall doors were shut.

'Eleanor?'

'Woohoo! That's me!'

One of the doors swung open and out flopped Eleanor, half-naked, her Fuck-You Dress up around her waist, and a total stranger in the cubicle, buttoning his trousers. Her Fuck-You Dress had morphed into a Fuck-Me Dress.

'What did you do to her?' I asked stupidly. For some reason my anger was directed at this total stranger.

He ignored me and strode out of the men's room. Eleanor was laughing.

'I needed that.' She was too drunk to know what she was doing. She shoved her dress down to its proper place.

'Oh, Eleanor. Did you at least use a condom?'

'I don't think there was time.' This was from Dudley, who flushed the toilet and emerged from the second occupied stall. 'But she did seem to enjoy it.'

'I did indeed!' Eleanor burst out laughing again and slapped Dudley on the back. I wanted to shove his head down a toilet.

'You can't write about this.'

'I read *your* piece. All gossip and gossip columnists are rude, hey? I couldn't help but take it personally.'

I couldn't bring myself to suck up to him, 'No, I guess you couldn't.'

'Now, what exactly is the etiquette of sex in a public toilet? See you in the funny papers, Manners Girl.' He smirked out the door.

'I have a sudden headache,' Eleanor whimpered at me.

'You'll need a whole lot of Aspirin tomorrow,' I said, dragging her through the door.

The next Saturday, Dudley's column came out, and there I was, dubbed 'Manners Girl,' all my exploits (not to mention Eleanor's) served up in his characteristically snarky tone. Big boss Bradley would not be amused.

CHAPTER THREE

Money

'I really want to have breakfast in the hotel!'
Missy had resorted to foot stomping.

The three of us had decided to escape for a long week-end away. Besides being an exercise in bonding, it answered our need to leave town after Dudley's skewering of us in the press. So there we were, standing in the lobby of this five-star hotel arguing over breakfast food. You see, Eleanor was a bit short on cash. After twice being publicly humiliated she had gone on a shopping binge. And after splurging on £300 shoes and a £2000 dress, she was now flat broke. Still, we needed to get out of town, so I picked up the tab for her. That's right, not rich Missy, me. Which brings us back to the foot stomping. I had suggested a greasy spoon down the street with a £3.95 breakfast special, Missy wanted the £10 eggs in the hotel. I had to be firm.

'I just think it's too expensive.'

Though I kept thinking that Missy would clue in, she really didn't get it.

'Fine, whatever.'

We settled into a booth at the admittedly less than atmospheric greasy spoon and ordered eggs, bacon and toast. The waitress was churlish, the coffee not too hot, and I'll admit the clientele was a little on this side of trucker, but how bad could the food be? After all, this weekend wasn't about gastronomy but about friendship.

Our steaming plates of eggs arrived, and Eleanor and I dove right in. Missy sulked. Playing with her food like a five-year-old, she poked at the fried eggs with her fork, letting the yolks run over the plate and get soaked up by the bread. She pretended to take a bite of bacon then tossed it down and made a frowny face. Great.

'Suddenly not hungry?' I couldn't help but become a bit bitchy, 'Good thing that you didn't order the £10 eggs florentine in the hotel.'

Missy shrugged.

Eleanor, for her part, seemed oblivious to Missy's fuss and gulped her coffee, 'Wonder if there are any good stores nearby?'

I wanted to scream that she had no money to shop, but instead I took the bill from the narky waitress and paid it. All of it. And Missy let me. I thought at least she'd say thank you, or better, apologize for behaving like a troll and cough up her share. But no, with her new-found riches there also seemed to come a matching set of entitlement and snobbery. For the rest of the weekend she was cool and distant, insisting on spending time in all the boutiques Eleanor and I couldn't afford but making us watch her buy, buy and buy. Now, I didn't begrudge her the money that came with her marriage, but I couldn't help thinking that she could be handling it with more grace.

But rich was far from my reality. While Eleanor was broke, I was in debt. Since landing my job at the magazine I'd been on a bit of a shopping bender myself. I had maxed out my cards. And now the bills had begun to pile up on my doorstep. Funny how it is with credit cards. Shopping is easy, but it always seems to cost so much more when you see it all added up in print, with 18% per annum. But that's what money was for, right?

Money

The Fabulous Girl may not know everything there is to learn in life, but one thing she is clear on is that she doesn't want to end up like the Victorian Fab Girl Lily Bart: poor and friendless. Of course, thankfully, much has changed since Edith Wharton wrote *The House of Mirth*; a woman need not rely on marriage and 'proper society' to keep herself cosy or, in the case of poor Lily, alive. The modern FG can earn her own keep, thank you very much. However, along with financial independence comes financial responsibility.

An important part of becoming a real grown-up is learning how to manage money. This is absolutely vital to the fully formed Fabulous Girl. Many women are not raised to be knowledgeable about, let alone assertive and creative with, money. Many, in fact, have inherited their mothers' ambivalence about finances. Not only does this mean a girl can't be as fabulous as she could be, it can also mean she puts herself at actual risk.

The first hurdle to overcome may be the Fabulous Girl's fear of finance. Numbers can terrify her. All through school she may have received bad marks in maths and so was convinced she was incapable of handling her money, a trait in her early twenties she thought was attractive in an 'oh, how sweet' kind of way – in the back of her mind she may have imagined some man would at least share the burden of all that icky financial stuff. Hah. All that happens to the finance-phobic FG is debt, maxed credit cards and overdrawn bank accounts. Surefire symptoms of the money-scared FG is that upon withdrawing cash from an ATM she tosses away the receipt – too anxious to see the balance and learn the truth – and at home her bills pile up unopened. These are the bad habits that any FG must learn to break.

We all know a woman needs a room of her own, but let's add to that a portfolio as well, shall we? No matter how much or how little she makes, an FG should have a financial plan. If she has very little there may seem to be no point in this. There is. You may have nothing at all to save, but just knowing where your money is being spent is a useful tool and a good habit to get into.

The Rich FG

With all of her talents, there may come a day when the FG is remunerated in a big way. This can manifest itself in many forms, from being able to buy a home for herself (and by herself) to quitting her job and becoming an integral part of the international jet set. How much money constitutes life-changing wealth varies with the individual Fabulous Girl. What doesn't vary from FG to FG is her gracious demeanour. Never a money flaunter, the Fabulous Girl may spoil her family, friends and, naturally, herself, but she does so in a way that doesn't scream 'filthy rich' but rather 'generous.' While non-FGs – say the newly crowned 'Miss Rich Bitch' – may turn to gaudy wardrobes, dripping gold jewellery and name-dropping here, there and everywhere, all the while snubbing their old friends, the FG acts as if little has changed – she just can afford nicer things.

Now, the FG with the sudden professional success is going to need new people in her life to help her.

The accountant
Once you move into a new income bracket, you need an accountant to help you deal with your riches. Depending on what field your success is in, try to find an accountant who is

familiar with the issues and tax laws associated with it. Ask other people in your field for recommendations.

The bank

Banks are not the place to find good manners. Whatever they may profess in their advertisements, most banks have little interest in individual accounts. You must be very assertive to get what you want out of any exchange with banks. Refuse to be treated like a child. Sadly, charm and warmth – two very useful elements in an FG arsenal – make very little difference within the walls of finance. An FG will get further employing a businesslike tone.

Even when she does assert herself in a reasonable way, an FG may find herself receiving less than acceptable service. At this point she needs to get tough. Let the person you're dealing with know exactly what you want and by when. If it's been a month since you applied for credit and you've left three unreturned calls to Bingo, the fourth should go like this: 'Hello, this is Ms Fab, your client. I came into your office on November eighth to apply for a line of credit. I have left 3 messages for you checking on the status of my application. I have not received a response from you. I need to hear back from you by the end of tomorrow before I assume that there is someone else I should be dealing with on this matter.' And if you don't hear back, call his manager and ask her to take over your application.

Investment firms

If an FG suddenly – or not so suddenly – has a lot of money to play with, she needs to find people to help her with the rules of the game. It's a very good idea to get a financial adviser on your team as soon as possible. There may be significant tax breaks you're missing out on by not discussing your new situation promptly.

Don't be afraid to seem dumb in these meetings. Ask whatever questions you need to be satisfied. Ask more than once if you still don't get it. Let your investor know how much you want to spend, what risk you're comfortable with, what your goals are. Listen to the advice offered, but don't forget to stand up for yourself. You may choose to sink all your savings into a house – even if your consultant advises against it. These people make money by keeping your money in the markets, not by your taking out a mortgage.

WHEN YOU ARE THE WEALTHIEST PERSON IN YOUR SOCIAL CIRCLE

An FG shouldn't have to feel guilty about her successes. She should enjoy them. If your winning streak is a recent one, it may be hard for the people around you to cope with the new you. This doesn't mean you have to accept rude treatment, however. It's not appropriate for people to intimate that your life is trouble-free now that you've hit the big time, even if things have been a little sweeter lately. Remarks like 'What do you care how much the bill is, you're rich' or 'Must be nice not to have to worry about money like the rest of us' are rude and make you feel bad whether they are intended to or not. The best response to such comments is to laugh them off rather than engaging in a conversation about money, or worse, getting defensive. If it goes any further than this, you should draw the line. 'Jokes' along the lines of 'Can I borrow twenty quid? No, really, can I borrow twenty quid?' shouldn't be tolerated. Be direct with the fool. 'Oh, I see, you're joking about the money that my last film made. Right. Actually, I only carry fifties now, so I guess I can't help you out.'

MONEY AND YOUR MATE

If you make a lot more than your mate, it can be stressful – for both of you. Although most modern couples don't expect the woman to be at home while the man is out hunting and gathering, there are still residual feelings that a man should make more than a woman. When this isn't true it can create tensions. Does he feel emasculated? Do you feel responsible for the both of you in a way that you're not comfortable with? When couples have very different incomes it is important for them to decide at what level they are going to live. Do you live at the level of the lower earner so that he can be an equal contributor? Or do you decide to supplement his standard of living by paying the lion's share of the mortgage or rent? Be honest about how the disparity makes both of you feel. If you are paying more, are you going to feel that he should then pick up more of the housecleaning duties? If you're living down to meet his income, is he going to feel that you could be making things more comfortable if you weren't holding out? Likewise, the FG may find herself feeling resentful about not enjoying the finer things that she can well afford. Whatever you decide, neither of you should refer to your financial discrepancy when it comes to decision making. The person with the bigger paycheque does not become the final word on all issues of conflict.

Joint accounts: should you?

This decision, made by every soon-to-be live-in or married couple, can be fraught. It is, in some respects, a question of trust. And of course, an FG trusts her mate – she's about to move in with him, right? From her experience and from the stories of others, however, the FG knows that everything can change and often does. We've all heard tales of the FG whose husband ran off with the au pair, only he decided he'd fund his escape by emptying out their joint account.

Every FG needs her privacy and a decent sum of her own money. In her grandmother's day it would have been called 'mad money' or 'rainy-day money.' Now let's call it three months' rent and one great dress. The Fabulous Girl needs to be in control of her own finances and make her own educated decisions about what she can and cannot afford. If all you have is a joint account then you will end up having needless discussions and resentments over your choice to buy those Prada pumps instead of the new DVD player. In other words, he needs *his* own cash, too. Why not have both? Have your own accounts and share one chequing account into which you each put money every month for rent, food, phone and utilities. This will mean sitting down and creating a shared budget. If the love of your life gets pushy about having only a joint account, stand your ground. It's your money and you need to be in charge. You will never regret sticking to this policy. Nor will you regret losing a lout if he's not willing to give you the freedom you need.

PUTTING YOUR MONEY WHERE YOUR MOUTH IS

It is terribly tiresome to be around a newly minted rich person who talks about nothing but money all the time. This is one of the reasons that the term *nouveau riche* is used with such derision by both the old-money and the no-money crowds. If someone you've just met compliments you on your silver cargo pants, you need only say thank you. You don't need to add, 'They're Balenciaga.' Consider this the rule of thumb: When elaboration is unnecessary, don't do it. 'I've been out of town' is the perfectly appropriate response to 'Where have you been lately?' Unless you're asked for details, which you probably will be, don't start with 'I've just come back from wintering in St Barts aboard the Casiraghi yacht . . .'

Besides the less you blather, the more intriguing you are. Everyone likes a good mystery, and you'll be a more desirable part of your new and old social settings if you appear well adjusted to your good fortune.

RICH FG, POOR FG

The Fabulous Girl who has more money must be aware that not all her friends are as wealthy as she is. An FG on a budget may not be able to dine at the finer restaurants or shop in the finer boutiques with her more well-heeled pals. The wealthy FG must also take into account different considerations in style and taste while socializing with her pals who have less. But isn't a large part of being a good friend making adjustments to suit others?

Freeloaders

Liggers, spongers – you know the type. This isn't your friend who's down on her luck, this is the person who simply doesn't want to part company with her moolah. You're out for drinks or dinner with a group of friends. The bill comes and everyone reaches for her handbag. Everyone except Miss Mean, that is. She forgot to go to the bank machine. She could have sworn she had a twenty in her purse this afternoon. Sure. Whatever. When this happens three times or more you are in the company of a Taker. Whether or not it's intentional, this person is a manipulator. Either she can't afford the same lifestyle as her friends but isn't willing to admit it, or she is just childish and exists in the delusion that somehow the world will always provide for her. You can still be friends with this person – although not close, let's-go for-pedicures-together-on-Saturday-afternoon-type friends – you just have to monitor what kind of activities you invite her to.

It's sometimes helpful to exaggerate things to clarify them. Let's say you bump into Miss Mean at a book launch. After an hour a group of pals decides to move on to dinner. Suggest a restaurant on the expensive side of what everyone is willing to spend. This will help the Meanie to think about her financial situation and beg off. If she doesn't and she tries to worm out of the bill, you may have to politely point out, with a hint of sarcasm, 'What a coincidence – there happens to be an ATM just on the corner.' Or sweetly offer to lend the Meanie the money and tell her she can pay you on the walk home by stopping at that very ATM. And do it.

PHILANTHROPY

There is an unfair and unkind perception of a certain kind of wealthy woman who gives to charity. The word *socialite* is often tossed around instead of *philanthropist*. Whether she makes her own fortune, married it or was born into it, a rich FG does not allow this perceived slight to hinder her generosity. When she makes money, she likes to give her friends gifts, treat them to dinners and so on. But she should also consider donating time and money to charity. While this may seem corny, there were no doubt many people who helped the FG on her way to the top, and supporting a cause is one way to give back. The Fabulous Girl is not afraid to make time to volunteer or to write a cheque. And there are numerous charities that will appeal to her: children, animals, the environment, medical research and art are all high on the FG's list of worthiness. On every level, giving money to charity is a good idea. It balances an FG's karma. It gives her a break at tax time. It establishes her in the web of society. The FG knows that part of the responsibilities and privileges of wealth is philanthropy. Altruism is definitely a part of the

FG vocabulary, and she encourages others to do the same by becoming involved in fundraising for charity.

SAVING

Do think about the future? Indeed, it is easier to be frugal now that you have a little cash. Somehow having even a little extra money allows you to look at your financial state more closely, more comfortably. Take advantage of this feeling of freedom and start putting money away. And not just in your current account either. Educate yourself on higher-earning places to put your money.

HAVING MONEY MEANS YOU NEED MORE MONEY

Life – and with it your expenses – does seem to have a way of expanding to eat up whatever your income is. More social invitations means you're eating out more. You want to look good, so you're shopping more. Be careful not to fall into the trap of comparing yourself too much with new, rich friends. It's intoxicating to suddenly have some money to toss around. And if you have wealthy friends it can be even more tempting. But don't be put off your own financial course.

Get advice from people who have been financially successful in your field. Learn what they did to adjust to their wealth. Did they incorporate? Making such inquiries is not rude or prying if done discreetly.

CREDIT CARD DENIED

You're trying to impress a new client. You've booked a table at a cool – but not intimidating – place. The night has gone well. You're pretty sure that Mr Rich is going to go back to his office tomorrow and recommend that they go with your firm. Your boss is going to be very pleased. By the end of the meal it seems all sewn up. You throw down your plastic for the waitress to scoop up. Only she comes back a minute later with a pitying look on her face: 'I'm sorry, your card has been declined.' Of course, you die inside. But you must act fast. Get up immediately, saying to your guests, 'I'd better just go and sort this out. I'll just be a moment.' Hopefully, you'll be dining in an establishment where the staff won't announce it at the table but rather will ask you to come with them to a more discreet spot.

If you can put the check on another credit or debit card, then obviously that's the simplest solution. If you don't have another credit card and they won't take a bank card, ask for the nearest bank machine. If it's close by, just run out, use it and pay the waitress in cash at the register (hopefully out of view of your guests). Then you can go back to the table and just shrug, 'All sorted out. Don't know what the trouble was.' The worst thing to do is to get embarrassed and flustered.

Actually, the *very* worst thing to do is ask your guests for money. If you don't have the cash in your account or there is no bank machine handy, you may be faced with this terrible prospect. Chances are, however, that you can call a friend, a very good friend, and ask her to pay the bill. Your friend should be able to use her credit card over the phone, but if not (or if she's also maxed out), arrange for her to come down to the bistro and pay the waitress directly with cash, again so that your clients are unaware.

The very, *very* worst case scenario may still happen: you can't get hold of a single flush friend. So you must explain the situation very plainly to your clients, express your embarrassment and let them pay. But send them the money the very next day along with a thank-you note and a promise to have dinner another time, on you!

The Poor FG

Rich is fun. Rich is good. Poor sucks. But most of us are more likely to be poor than we are to be rich. Poor, however, doesn't mean that one does without every fabulous necessity, or that one can't climb out of the rut that often befalls the indebted and the low income earner.

BITTERNESS

You may be poor because of your chosen profession. It's unfair that modern dancers make less than lawyers or that poets make less than accountants. It's also unfair of the world to treat you as if you are less valuable because you work in a profession that doesn't pay well. But just as it's not your fault that you don't make a lot of money, so it is not the fault of the high earner that she does. It is the height of bad manners to make cracks about people's worth based on their income – no matter if they're rich or poor. There exists a false logic that says that if a person makes a lot of money, he must have duped the world and is necessarily crass and shallow. This is as unfair an assumption as thinking that all modest earners are lazy slackers.

THE BUDGET FABULOUS GIRL:
HOW TO SAVE AND STILL BE FABULOUS

The Fabulous Girl likes eating out. She gets invited out a lot. But the number-one budget killer is a consistent diet of restaurant fare. If you are in a serious or not-so-serious financial crunch, the best thing you can do is to stop dining out. You don't have to be obvious about it if you'd rather not make a public announcement about your situation. Instead you can start inviting friends over to your place for dinners.

Although it costs more than only feeding yourself, it is still much cheaper than a restaurant bill. Another tactic is to agree to meet for a cocktail, or any other activity, rather than a meal. People with active social lives tend to get lazy about how they hang out with friends. You'd have a good time going to a gallery with a friend and it's cheaper than the little French bistro you normally frequent.

Fabulous Girl tip: Working lunch

By this we don't mean simply working at your desk while you throw back some sushi. The FG knows how to work her lunch to save some money. How? By bringing her lunch to work every day. Sure, making your own sandwiches isn't glamorous, but the FG may save herself at least £25 per week on lunches alone. This means £100 a month is saved and that's a lot of money. And let's face it, most takeaway lunches aren't worth the money anyway, so why not take the cash? Don't be deceived into thinking that £5 each lunch hour doesn't add up.

The other working lunch

The other way to keep your lunch expenses down is to time your appointments around noon. Of course, you must be meeting with someone who is obliged to pick up the tab – a client or anyone you are working for. It sounds crafty, but if you suggest meeting someone at noon they will almost always come back with 'Let's make it a lunch.'

THE FG SPLURGE

One thing that the financially conscious FG should avoid is the splurge, especially the impulse splurge. When shopping, it is tempting to dive into designer boutiques; however, such trips can also be a painful reminder of your lack of funds.

Some FGs are able to window shop and browse without incident; others may fall prey to the splurge instinct. This occurs when the FG, say, tries on a pair of very pricey Italian-made trousers. They fit like a glove – in fact, for all intents and purposes it appears they were made just for her. Satisfied, she removes them only to check the price tag: £400. A tidy sum for anyone, most of all the non-rich FG. But she wants them, she really wants them. Her heart begins to race. She gets dizzy as she concludes that her life won't be complete without them. She envisions herself striding into a chic party wearing the trousers, cutting a figure of feminine independence and mystery, taking a meeting with a soon-to-be-big client who sees her as capable and creative, landing that dream job because of her take-charge attitude – all contingent on these trousers. She may as well leave her job and wear pyjamas every day if she can't have those trousers. Then she remembers she has room on her credit card – it's about all the room available on the card, but, hey.

This is when the FG must do the impossible: she must put the pants back on the rack and march out of the store immediately. She can at the very most put them on hold until the next day, but she cannot buy them then and there. She needs the splurge fever to subside. Ninety-nine per cent of the time it will. The FG will come to her senses and know in her heart that she can't afford them and that, really, her life is meaningful without them, albeit a little less perfect. If in the next twenty-four hours the feeling doesn't subside, then she can go and visit the trousers, but if the FG doesn't wait then she will have the big gulp of guilt as soon as she brings her impulse buy home. And an even worse anxiety attack when the bill arrives.

Losing It All

It can happen to any Fabulous Girl. You toiled away for years as a jazz singer, hoping for your big break. One glorious day a record label exec happened upon your show and signed you then and there. Of course the fact that the record company doesn't produce jazz albums didn't seem to matter. You went along with the producer's vision and lo and behold you cut a techno-pop CD. You really can't stand the sound, but it hit number one in the week. The album made you very, very rich.

This kind of sudden wealth can make you tempted to spend in an easy-come, easy-go way. This isn't uncommon. Many famous Fabulous Girls have gone broke by buying too much too fast (or by having bad managers). And you may discover that money isn't that easy to earn – your second album bombed. If you find yourself in the sad situation of having blown through £3 million in two years, you have little choice but to pick yourself up and start all over again. What's done is done. Is it embarrassing? Yes it is. Will you get over it? Hopefully. Will you get rich again? Maybe.

Once you've had money it's difficult to go back. You may feel as if you are the kind of person who *should* have money (and an FG does rich well!), and so it can be very difficult to accept your reversal of fortune. But you must. It is dangerous to keep living at your old, more affluent level because you are too prideful to acknowledge the change in your life. Rather than revealing your financial woes, just tell people that you need to keep it real right now and that you want to get back to your jazz roots.

Selling your life

Unfortunately, going broke means that, to make ends meet, you may have to part company with things you love. Your beloved Warhol silkscreen must go to Sotheby's. Selling off pieces of your life is an emotional ordeal. No matter how many times you tell yourself, 'They're just material possessions' these articles represent your life and often have deep sentimental value. The best thing to do is to sell what you must and sell it to strangers. You don't want to walk into an acquaintance's home one evening to see your Warhol hanging on their tacky wood-panelled wall.

Friends should take note: if someone in their lives is forced to purge her assets, then 'Oh, I saw your Warhol sell at auction for three times what you got for it' is not welcome news. Neither does it help to remark, 'At least you have a Warhol to sell.'

There is little sympathy for the newly impoverished FG. She will learn the hard way that society tends to resent those with money. Some people are only too gleeful, despite surface pretensions, to watch a wealthy person fall to a lower level (all the more reason to handle your wealth with quiet grace when you do have it). Of course, this sets the stage for a great comeback, yet another fave story for the public to latch onto. The FG will ride the highs and lows with equal panache.

Debt

Face it. If you have a sudden shift in fortune you may find yourself with a debt load that you cannot comfortably handle. Maybe you built up debt when you were making more money and now you're drowning in it, or you just

107

finished at university and now you have a Masters degree and a huge bill. The worst thing you can do is go into denial. Terrifying as it is, you must look clearly at how much you owe. Have a friend over to help you through this. FGs have been known to sit with their debt-addled friends, a stack of bills and a bottle of red wine and help them face the music. Open the bills, make a list of the amounts, add it all up and make a plan. Call the people you owe money to. If you speak to creditors before they have to come after you things will go much better.

COLLECTION AGENCIES

People who work for collection agencies are the meanest people alive: those nasty phone callers employed by collection agencies to terrorize you. Once a debt has been handed over to a collection agency, you have little recourse but to deal with the agency over the outstanding bill. Although you are clearly in a position of weakness, try to keep up a professional manner with these people. Be firm about negotiating a reasonable pay-back schedule with them. Even if at the moment you can only offer to give them £10 a month, make that offer. They may cancel your credit card, but if you are making an offer to them rather than refusing to pay then generally they'll work with you.

Remember that if creditors cash your cheque, they cannot sue you or claim you aren't paying enough. If you pay them nothing or they refuse your payment you may find that the collection agency begins to garnish money from your pay-cheque. If this happens you need to get a credit counsellor on board and you may even end up going to court to remove the garnishment.

BAD CREDIT RATING

If you suspect that you have a bad credit rating you probably do. Again, it's better to face the music than to cower in the corner. You have a right to see your credit rating. You can apply through various agencies to see it. You will be assigned a number which rates you to potential lenders. You can also see who has ratted you out as a bad credit risk. Deal with these people first: clear your debt with them as soon as possible. Many creditors automatically report you to the credit bureau as soon as a single payment has been missed or is even late. Find out which credit cards or bills work this way. Even if you can only pay less than the minimum on these debts, do it. If you're worried about it, phone in and report your payment or the fact that you're going to be late so that you're not reported to the credit bureau.

You can improve your credit rating by – obviously – paying off your bills. But you can also improve it by taking out a small amount of credit and making regular payments on it. It's difficult to get credit, but it does wonders for your credit rating so it's worth the effort.

BANKRUPTCY

There may come a time that you are so seriously in the hole that you can't possibly dig yourself out. This is what bankruptcy laws are for. If you declare bankruptcy, you won't be able to get a credit card or loan for an extended period of time. Again, hire professional help. An insolvency lawyer can help you file for bankruptcy, but there are also debt counsellors who can see you through the process and help stop those harassing collection agency phone calls. You also do not have to announce to anyone in your circle that you are bankrupt.

The bills kept coming, credit cards from the bank and from my favourite department stores. I could not resist them, neither could I pay them. I had three months of bills creating a mountain on my kitchen counter, all unopened. Somewhere along the way I had neglected to make even the minimum monthly payment. I don't know what had come over me, but those daunting white envelopes terrified me. The trouble was I didn't know how to manage my monthly income. When I was freelancing I couldn't get credit, so it was never an issue. But as soon as I had a real job, I became legitimate in the eyes of all the shops and banks, and they were throwing cards at me like confetti. I became their prisoner. I tried to pay down chunks at a time, but between rent and restaurants, I just couldn't make a dent in it. Every time I withdrew cash from an ATM I would toss away the receipt, unable to look at the balance.

I was managing to exist in this state of extreme financial ignorance until one night, as I was sitting at home cuddled in Nice's arms, Kitty at my feet, the phone rang. It was a bill collector. In one of those nasty envelopes had been a letter warning me that if I didn't pay up, the bill would be sent to a collection agency. Of course, not having opened any of those letters, how would I know such a thing was possible?

I tried to whisper into the phone. Nice didn't know

about my situation, and I was hoping to keep it that way.

The man on the end of the phone, however, was mean and rude. He wouldn't listen to me. In answer to his threats, I promised to pay the bill the next day, knowing full well I didn't have the money. When I hung up, Nice was suspicious.

'Everything okay?'

'Just fine,' I lied. 'That was the production department at the magazine. They need my copy earlier than normal.'

The calls kept coming, both at work and at home. It was awful. Still I kept my worries to myself, living paycheque to paycheque, making deals with the devilish collection agencies and not living up to them. I probably would have gone on like this indefinitely, or at least until someone sued me, if it hadn't been for the shower.

I was in the shower when one of those bastards called, and Nice answered my phone. He didn't usually answer my phone, but this time he did. And the collection guy left a rather detailed message. I tried to be angry with Nice, figuring I'd distract him with an argument about privacy, but he wouldn't listen.

'You should have told me about this, I could have helped you.'

'I can handle it myself. I'm just a bit behind.'

'A bit? Let me give you the money. We can consolidate your debt—'

'No.'

I just couldn't stand the thought of being in debt to my boyfriend – it was a point of pride. It took a while, but finally Nice did take 'no' for my answer. It had been an exhausting fight and we had parted angrily. That, however, was the least of my worries. Nice was right – I needed to pay off the bills and only have one payment. I couldn't get a bank loan; the less-than-helpful manager had said I was too risky. Boy, did I hate banks. So I called Missy.

'How much do you need?'

I told her, waited for a lecture, a scream or something. She was silent.

'I know I can pay you back.'

I could hear her breathing at the end of the line. Perhaps I had pushed our friendship too far. I'm not sure how I would have reacted in her shoes: money does do strange things to people.

'Okay, I'll write you a cheque.'

Missy had one condition to her loan: I had to learn to budget. She came over one night, wine bottle in hand, and we systematically opened up every bill I had accumulated, tallied it up and then Missy gave me the money.

It was simple. I was freed from the evil creditors, and Missy seemed happy to help. As a thank you I invited Missy out for breakfast – at a five-star hotel, of course. When the bill came I naturally reached for it. But Missy beat me to it.

'It's on me.'

I resisted. After all, I wanted to thank her for the help. But she wouldn't hear of it. That was the last time Missy or I ever mentioned the loan. I simply paid her back an agreed-upon amount every month. She was much more gracious than any banker.

CHAPTER FOUR

Friendship

'What can I get you ladies to drink?'

Missy, Eleanor and I were in celebration mode and had met at our favourite haunt, Dominick's. It was a homely Italian place that still did the whole red-and-white-checked-tablecloth thing but somehow always attracted a youngish crowd. It's strange that the place where Missy and I had slaved as waitresses just a couple of years ago had now become our local, but there you go. We were always model customers and tipped the waitresses generously.

'Champagne for the table,' Missy ordered. She was obviously in a money's-no-object mood.

Exactly what we were celebrating wasn't clear. It had been about two months since the whole Bingo-Mel-Dudley affair, and life had pretty much glided by without incident. Eleanor had decided it was time to move forward with her life and had suggested a girls' night out.

'I'm ready for new challenges.'

'And new men,' I suggested hopefully, as Eleanor had a long history of getting back together with Bingo no matter what the indiscretion on his part, though thankfully this last time seemed to be sticking.

The champagne arrived, an extravagance that only Missy could afford, but since she was paying I made sure the waiter filled my glass to the brim.

'Should we make a toast?' I thought it was the simplest of

questions with a straightforward 'Cheers'. as the answer.

Eleanor raised her glass: 'I'm pregnant.' She sipped just enough bubbly to wet her lips. 'That's my last taste for the next seven months.'

I looked at Missy. Had she known? Missy stared at me. Obviously, this was news to her too. The two of us sat dumbly with our flutes raised.

'Um, you going to drink that?' Eleanor looked a bit annoyed.

'Congratulations,' I spurted out.

'Holy shit,' was Missy's well-thought-out response.

'I know, my doctor only confirmed it this morning.'

'How do you feel?' I asked.

'Oh, forget her feelings! Are you going to keep it? And who's the father?' Missy demanded. 'That's what we really want to know.'

'Actually, yes, I am going to keep it.'

'That's huge, Eleanor.'

'But the father will remain a secret, for now.'

'You're *choosing* to be a single mum?' Missy had a knack for stating the most terrifying facts out loud.

'It won't be that bad. My mum can help. I have a good job with great benefits.'

'I wouldn't raise a kid on my own, not in this city.'

I wanted to quietly wring Missy's neck.

'Have you thought of adoption?'

'Missy!' I couldn't stay silent. 'Eleanor, this is very exciting, you know we're both here for you. Missy and I are just in a state of shock. Why didn't you say anything?'

'Denial.'

We continued with our celebratory dinner, discussing the usual: men, books, work and now, baby stuff. To tell the truth, in my quest for career I hadn't spent much time thinking about children. They were cute but messy, lovable but loud. Now there was going to be one in my closest circle of friends. But that wasn't the thing that got me. I still couldn't help but wonder if the stranger in the bathroom had knocked Eleanor up. Or was it Bingo? I suspected that my scariest thought was somehow closer to reality; Eleanor didn't know who the father was. There was only one way to find out for sure.

'Does Bingo know?'

'Haven't told him,' Eleanor evaded my attempt at sneakiness.

'Should he know?' Missy was on to my plan.

'Not from either of you.' With that Eleanor continued cutting into her rare steak.

Friends

The Fabulous Girl has many friends and acquaintances. They are, after all, a necessity for a thriving social life and are also a much-needed support network. The FG herself is a good friend. However, as in any intense relationship, there may be pitfalls. The Fabulous Girl recognizes that the people who matter most to her are sometimes the greatest disappointments and can unfortunately be the recipients of her poorest behaviour. There will be occasions when the FG's friendships are tested or even ruined. To navigate these extremes of friendship, the Fabulous Girl must learn the skill of grace under pressure.

Meow

There are few relationships in life as complicated as best gal-pals. Women are often heard to exclaim that their friendships with their girlfriends are much more secure, honest, trustworthy and longlasting than relationships with the opposite sex. Is there any woman who hasn't wished her relationships with men were as solid as those with women? However, the flip side of intense female friendships can be less than ideal.

Women, sorry to say, can be capable of treating their friends in an unfair and thoroughly rude manner. You know the scene. There you are with your two best friends. You gab, you drink, you eat, you share secrets, and then it happens: one of you gets up to use the washroom and the remaining pals launch into a bitchfest behind the absent one's back. 'I just don't know why Esther can't get her life together . . . she can be so stupid sometimes.' 'Did you see what she's wearing today? She just doesn't have the legs for that mini . . .'

The Fabulous Girl will think carefully about what she says

118

about her friends while they're out of the room. She is aware that no matter what her own code of conduct is, she can never prevent others from dissing her. Still, she can set an example of discretion.

The FG follows these steps toward thwarting cattiness:

1. Never say something critical about a friend that you wouldn't have the nerve to say face to face under the right conditions.

2. An easy way to avoid the gossip habit is to not catch up on the details of Pal A's life while chatting with Pal B. Don't ask Alice how Mabel is doing, ask Mabel. It's a slippery slope from 'Mabel's still having a hard time at her new job' to 'Why doesn't she grow a backbone?'

3. If you've been hurt or angered by a friend's behaviour, go ahead and ask a mutual friend his or her opinion about how best to approach the situation. But don't use the third friend merely as a sounding board for your rants. The person you really need to be speaking to is the friend who hurt your feelings.

4. If you're jealous of a friend, better to admit it than to say disparaging things about her to others in the hopes of diverting attention away from her and toward yourself.

5. Try loyalty instead. When others are getting nasty about your friend, nip it in the bud. Tell them what a great friend Mabel is and that you simply don't want to participate in catty behaviour. It's best to let people know right away your connection to the person they're dissing so they don't feel stupid when they realize it later.

6. If all else fails, change the subject. Or just walk away from the catty conversation.

7. If you know that a friend has been talking about you behind your back, you may decide you need to confront her. As calmly as you can, ask your friend what's up. Give her a

chance to explain herself – after all, you've probably only heard a piece of gossip and you know how unreliable that can be. You may be angry at and hurt by your friend, but by remaining calm you will be showing your friend that it is better to come to you directly with a problem than to mouth off about it with someone else.

Competition Among FGs

Another real issue between women is competitiveness. Few women like to admit that they experience these feelings – we're raised to believe it's just not nice. However, this competitiveness does exist. There are many different types, and they can occur between the best of friends, total strangers and mortal enemies.

THE LOOK CONTEST

One of the mildest forms of competition occurs in the world of socializing. Women are often competitive at parties and other social events, each trying to look her best while checking out the other females to see who's got the best dress, shoes, hair and so on, each one calculating silently where she herself lands on the evening's sex-appeal scale. That old saying that 'women dress for each other' is not without truth. But that's the fun part of being female – and of being a Fabulous Girl. FGs don't shrink from this type of competition. How many women friends call each other before attending a 'do' to find out what the other is wearing? It's all part of friendly, supportive camaraderie, in a 'let's both wear our miniskirts' way. Of course, while FGs save each other from fashion emergencies, this is also a way of gearing her own look for the night. She may think to herself, 'Betty is wearing black again – I'll wear red and really stand out.' This actually isn't ungracious but a natural reaction to wanting to be noticed. Sure Betty may turn up and say, 'Ooh, I should really wear colour.' But you know that each FG will sincerely tell the other, 'You look great,' and enter the party armed with the confidence that this type of female bonding brings.

BEST FRIEND

Best friends have many levels to their relationship. And it is natural, especially if they are in similar fields, for them to be competitive. Even if this is not explicit, there may be a current running below the surface. Hopefully, that's where it stays. This kind of competition can be motivating. If you see that your close friend has just accomplished something great – started her own business, produced a play – it can drive you to work harder in your own life. But be careful if you and your friend are in the same line of work not to pay more attention to her career than yours. Spending too much time playing the comparison game can close you off to opportunities in your own life. Don't be so busy trying to accomplish what your friend has that you don't realize your own genuine goals.

If you find yourself in an actual competition with a good friend – say, you're up for the same job – you need to talk about it. Remind yourselves that although this is an awkward situation, the final decision does not belong to either of you – it's out of your hands. Obviously, you would only go forward in this kind of competition if the goal is something you truly want. Check that you don't want the job just because your friend wants it. This is especially true if you know your friend is applying for a job but you proceed with it anyway. Unless it is the job opportunity of a lifetime, there is something underhanded about throwing in your own resumé after you know she's told you she really wants it.

WOLF IN FG CLOTHING

Friendships are so important to FGs – particularly her friendships with other women – that she puts a great deal of herself into them. If she is disappointed by a friendship, it can come as a terrible blow. The worst kind of letdown that can afflict an FG comes when a woman pretends to be a friendly, FG-style girly-girl only to be revealed as a back-stabbing man-poacher. It's one thing to cope with someone who makes no bones about being after your man – you can deal with this kind of wench. It's not easy, but you can deal with it.

Far more complicated and difficult to recognize is the faux friend. Perhaps she even fools herself into thinking she wants a friendship with you. Whatever. When you first make the acquaintance of this woman it is probably in the company of other women, where she seems like an entirely likeable person. She's so warm and winning that you start to think how lucky you are to have a new friend. You'll start to notice, though, that she makes you uncomfortable in the presence of your man. She makes eyes at him, touches him too much, maybe even tries to make social contact with him that excludes you. At first the FG will try to rationalize her pal's behaviour: she's being a good friend by getting to know Mr Nice better. But then your boyfriend admits to you that he's getting uncomfortable with the way she's been calling him at his office. A teeny bit of research will likely uncover a history of poaching on the part of this woman.

The FG is a busy woman and has no time for this kind of faux friend. While a thorough snubbing is not necessarily in order, all friendly overtures on the FG's part can stop. If the faux friend wants to know why you're not available for afternoon tea the way you used to be, you can be honest. Otherwise, the simplest thing is to just stop calling, stop making plans and keep conversations with her at parties to a minimum. In all likelihood, she'll barely notice – it was never you she was interested in anyway.

ENEMY GIRL

It usually begins in friendship. Or at least in acquaintanceship. But then you have a falling out. She asks your man out on a date while you're out of town, she bad-mouths you to a potential employer and then applies for the job herself, she repeats the secret she has sworn to keep. Whatever it is, you realize that this girl wishes you ill. And now you, the FG, have a mortal enemy. Yet if you are in the same social circle you are bound to see her all the time. You know that at every cocktail party, BBQ or birthday dinner (for a mutual friend) she will try to outdo you. Being an FG, you know her plan and are compelled to foil it. Every opportunity you have to look the part of the head turner you must jump on, even if you're not sure that she's going to be there. You can't let your guard down. The key to this situation is to remember that it is a *competition*, and no amount of telling yourself or your friends 'I don't care what she does, she's only making a fool of herself' will change that fact. So when you are dismissing her pettiness in public, you are also wearing killer heels, sporting great hair and smiling all the while.

It may seem anti-fabulous to endorse a course of steely competition, but really we are talking about pride here. If an FG has to find a way to coexist with the enemy girl then being better – better dressed, better behaved, and so on – will give the FG the confidence to face these awkward situations.

The FG wins the competition because she is sophisticated and silent about her grudge against the enemy girl. The first sign of victory is when one woman is caught dissing the other or, worse, bragging loudly about herself (especially within earshot of the other).

If, on a rare occasion, your enemy verbally attacks you, do as one FG did when her enemy girl called her trashy and slutty in front of mutual acquaintances: laugh in her face. This only makes the enemy look really, really bad.

When Good Friends Get It All

If she's not doing so fabulously in life, then when others become instantly famous or rich an FG can be taken aback. For some inexplicable reason, hanging out with friends or lovers who have always been successful doesn't have the same bite as a pal with new-found luck. It may be that the FG simply wasn't prepared, or perhaps there was some codependence going on in the relationship. A bit of that we'll-never-get-it-together-type sentiment. So that when only one of you (and *not* the FG) actually does make it big, it stings.

There is no point in pretending that this doesn't hurt or that jealousy is all bad. In fact the FG will rise to the occasion to celebrate with her friend, even hosting a small party or toasting at a celebratory dinner at the friend's favourite bistro. Then our FG will use the jealousy to examine her own goals and move forward with her own plans.

However, it is not appropriate to use that celebratory dinner as an opportunity to announce your plans to others. This will come across as a rather pathetic form of stealing someone else's thunder – never a fabulous move. And what FG would desire the pity of others who will see right through this tactic? An FG must know when to step into the limelight and when to bow out. Of course, the gracious successful friend, if she is an FG, will recognize the difficulty of your feelings and at some point will shift the attention over to you.

Adversity can bring out either the best or the worst in the FG. Yes, it is true, an FG can make poor judgment calls or act in a less than fabulous manner toward her friends and adversaries. However, she tries her best not to, and if she does she will apologize for her indiscretion. Sometimes in apologizing to her wounded friend she can open up about her negative feelings.

Don't Demote the Dumped

Your pal was dumped and it was a hard one. Being a good friend, you know you have to be there for her. You let her cry on your shoulder, you take her shoe shopping, and send her e-mails at work to check on her. But if you are in a relationship yourself, you might be tempted to do something else: demote her. That's right, often a dumped girl finds herself invited out to more brunches and matinees instead of the dinner and cocktail parties that she used to get asked to as half of a couple. Not fabulous. Part of the pain of a breakup is the way it shifts a social circle – she doesn't see his friends or family anymore, she doesn't have him as a buffer with her more boring old friends – so the worst thing you can do as a friend is add to these changes. Singleness is not a contagious disease, and your coupled friends will manage just fine in the presence of your newly single friend. Trust that she won't bring the party down with her sadness. If anything, her recent drama will add some fizz to your next party.

Your Friends and their Bad Ideas

We've all heard them – those brilliant ideas that sometimes seize friends, the same ideas that you know immediately are a *really* big mistake. Are we powerless to sway our friends? The Fabulous Girl must learn to distinguish between life-altering decisions where an intervention is required and harmless whims where it's best to keep your glossed lips shut.

EXTREME FRIENDS
Okay, so your best friend, who was dumped by her fiancé last week, has decided to leave her job as a florist and join the military. What's an FG to say? In a case of such poor judgement, you really must be honest, but not in a sarcastic, desperate way ('Are you *nuts*?'). Instead, try 'I think you should give this decision a few months – after all, in the twenty years I've known you you've never mentioned the army as a career choice.' You may even go so far as to suggest that her choice of life change may have more to do with being hurt than with national pride.

WHIMS
Every woman at some point in her life may get caught in a whimsical moment. Your friend spent ten days in the country, and boom, she sold her twentieth-floor flat and bought a bungalow in the middle of Nowhereville? Hmmm. When things seem to be heading down a dangerous path, you may of course express your feelings, but you may only do so *before* the decision has been made. Once that flat is sold, back off and be supportive. She'll feel bad enough asking to sleep on your sofa when she's back searching for a place in the city next year.

ENGAGEMENTS

There are certain situations, however, when a more traditional intervention is appropriate. Marriage is a very serious undertaking. It can be the death of all things fabulous in a girl's life if she chooses to pair up with the wrong man. Obviously, one never knows for sure if someone else's marriage will work. But occasionally it is blatantly obvious to an FG that her dear friend's marriage is doomed to fail. It is at this moment that an FG must be more forward. This is especially true if it's a second marriage. If your girlfriend isn't taking the act of matrimony seriously or the bloke is really a rebound relationship or for whatever reason you see a collision course, then you may need to figuratively tie your friend to a chair and perform the Spanish Inquisition. Some questions that may be of help:

- I thought you didn't believe in marriage?
- You've only known Fritz for six weeks – perhaps you should wait?
- Have you considered living together first?
- Have you fully considered what 'I do' means, versus merely thinking, 'I'll try'?
- How is this time going to be different from your first marriage?

At the very least, you'll get her to think. Of course, as mentioned before, it is easy when in love to justify anything, so the cagey FG friend must express her concerns without appearing to be entirely down on her friend's relationship.

Health Issues

We do live in a world of luxury and excess, and therefore

temptations are readily available to us all. Alcohol, drugs and even food can get the better of even the most 'together' friend. If someone you care for is actually in crisis, then you should push her to seek help. For example, if she is over-weight to a health-threatening degree – and by that we don't mean she's now a size 16, then that really does warrant a one-on-one conversation. Ask gently if everything is going well in her life, explain that you're concerned that she doesn't appear to be taking care of herself anymore. She may be depressed and in need of some help.

In these health situations, the Fabulous Girl can be there only as a friend. Unless she herself is a doctor, she can't pretend to diagnose her friend's trouble. How forceful the FG can be is determined by how close a friend or relation she is. With a more casual friendship, the FG can only suggest professional help; with her best friend of twenty years, the FG may have to shove her into her car and drive her to a detox centre, risking the friendship but knowing it's the right thing to do anyway.

DIET ETIQUETTE

If your friend is trying hard to lose weight and is doing so gradually, then be supportive. Ask her if she wants to be shielded from your snacking (at work or at home). While you would normally offer up a slice of cake or biscuit if you were going to have one yourself, refrain from asking your pal if that is her wish.

The Taker

The phrase 'ask and you shall receive' is often true when a good friend needs a favour. Have to borrow £20? A ride to the airport? Cat sitting? That great dress of yours for her first date with *him*? FGs don't mind doing the odd favour for their friends. It's when the same person asks the same person for help time and again that it enters ligger territory. If you happen to be going through a needy stage in your life, parcel out the favour asking. And keep in mind the size of the favour. There is a difference between 'May I sleep on your sofa tonight?' and 'Can I borrow your Land Rover for the weekend?'

While the Fabulous Girl prides herself on being a loyal friend, she doesn't have to be a pushover. Remember, *decorum* doesn't mean *doormat*. If you're not comfortable with what you're being asked, then say that little word: no.

It may seem adolescent to say that some people will only befriend you for what they can get out of you, but in the real world this happens all too often. The Taker is fairly easy to spot on the social landscape. If someone seems to be your buddy only because you keep lending her stuff or introducing her to the right people or inviting her to the right parties, then she needs to be cut off. If you're unsure, say no and observe. The Taker is never interested in a reciprocal friendship, where you are welcome to borrow her brand-new boots that she's never worn. Oh no, that would be the sole right of the Taker. The Fabulous Girl is never afraid of losing the Taker as a friend.

The Down-on-her-luck Friend

There will always be one friend who is forever in a state of ruin and despair. Sometimes it is a legitimate concern, a lost job or inability to find employment. 'It must be nice' or 'I wish I had your problem' is a sure sign of someone in your circle being down on her luck. These comments may sting you and make you defensive, but really they say far more about the state of mind of the person who said them than about you.

If the person is making efforts to change her situation then she should be supported. Encourage her, ask her how she is doing when you see her. But if she is interested in what you're up to, then you shouldn't edit your life for her either.

Some people, however, are just complainers. Don't get sucked into the drama suggested by their whining. For the complainer, these repeated refrains are like drawing breath. You may point out, 'Wow, you've been unhappy about your apartment for a while now.' If they don't at least admit this is a chronic problem, then in the future you need only acknowledge her crabbing and then change the subject.

When Other Friends Are Feuding

If you're stuck between two good friends who are fighting over something – man, job, whatever – you must be firm with them or else you'll wind up in the middle of the scuffle.

Don't take sides. Really. Tell each of them that you will not choose or form an opinion as to who is right or wrong.

Don't mediate. Listening to them rant about each other for too long may tempt you to try to make them see the light. You want them to see that they don't need to be feuding. But again, you're being forced into their fight, and often you are being used to fan the flames.

Don't discuss it. Pronounce that you will not tolerate their bad-mouthing each other in your presence. That you like them both and intend to remain friends with them both and that they'll have to work it out for themselves. This will

ensure that when they do patch things up you're not the one
suddenly on the outs.

When You're the Loser

Every Fabulous Girl will at some time encounter crisis in her
life. Things just aren't working out – your career as a
pharmaceutical sales-person isn't as glamorous as you'd
thought, you despise your colleagues but like your job, you
just can't stand your mate, everything he does is wrong. The
worst of it is, you realize that you're stuck in neutral with this
issue. All you can seem to do is fixate on your unhappiness.
An FG must recognize that repeated whining about a
particular problem will wear thin on the ears of even her best
friends. How many times can you complain to friends before
you either shut up or make some changes? For major life-
altering decisions, it can take months or years to actually
come to some conclusions. And rightly so if what you're
deciding is, say, to get a divorce. But in order for friends to
remain sympathetic and actually keep listening to you, you
must make efforts to improve your lot. You'll know that
you've reached the limit of a pal's patience when she stops
asking you for updates on your job or marital conundrum, or
if her comments become blunt: 'Bill's never going to leave his
wife for you, so why stick around?'

The Pryer

The sixties gave the Western world a great deal: good music,
great fashion and the Pill. Coupled with this freedom is the
notion that everyone is entitled to an opinion. The old saying
goes that politics and religion shouldn't be discussed in good

company – but there are many more things that should never, ever be spoken of. All FGs will avoid the following questions, and if asked themselves will politely decline to answer.

'ARE YOU STRAIGHT?'

One FG was asked this during a phone query with an estate agent. Put off her game by the off-putting question, she stammered out her answer. This let the agent feel free to rant about how there weren't many of 'them' in the neighbourhood. Questions from mere acquaintances about sexual preference, paternity, income or religion are wholly inappropriate. What to do when confronted with such rude enquiries? Simple. 'Excuse me?' usually works. It forces the other person to explain why he or she is asking such a personal question and it is often enough to make the offender back off. If the questioner persists, you are free to say you feel that it is none of their business.

'ARE YOU PREGNANT?'

Never, ever ask a woman if she's pregnant. A smiling 'Nope, just fat' in response will shut people up and teach them to never make that mistake again.

'ARE YOU TIRED?'

What this really means is 'You look tired,' and that's just not nice. Anyway, the answer is obviously yes – isn't everyone always tired?

'ARE YOU TWO GETTING MARRIED?'

Have you ever known people who are engaged to keep the news to themselves? No, we thought not. When people decide to get married they tend to tell people. Or they tell someone who tells everyone. When people (and let's face it, they tend to be married people) ask whether you and your mate are getting married, what they really mean is 'Why aren't you getting married?' Feel free to ask them, with a sweet smile on your face, whether they are still having sex.

'WHAT WERE YOU THINKING?'

Though it may seem customary for friends and relatives to mouth off with personal opinions on intimate life decisions, only when solicited are you free to give your opinion. Here's the standard rule: Did your pal ask you what you think of her purple dye job? Is she telling you she just did it, or that she is going to do it? If it's a done deal, keep your mouth shut.

'IF YOU WANT MY OPINION . . .'

Quit with this little number. People who ask this are forcing others to hear them out. Making friends listen politely to your opinion is not what a well-mannered person does. So don't be offended if your friend says, 'No, I've already made up my mind. Thank you.' If you are on the receiving end of unwanted advice, end the conversation. Restate your choice or decision and leave it at that. Do not fall into the trap of asking your opinionated friend why she hates the name Maria.

'ARE YOU LOSING WEIGHT?'

Even if the answer is yes, when asked in a group this can be very embarrassing, drawing unwanted attention to the person's body. If you want to say something positive, try 'You're looking great.'

POLITE PRYING

If you really must know why your best friend named her child Chadwick, then ask *how* she chose the name. Asking a question is always better than launching into a lengthy diatribe on the problem of bringing up kids in the city or buying a loft or 4 x 4. Forcing your opinions may only clam up your friends, who are going to do what they want anyway.

Men

The little dears can often be a cause of tension between women. Accordingly, there are certain rules of decorum an FG must follow when she and a friend are both attracted to the same man. Whoever spots him first has first dibs on seeking his attention. However, if his attention, once sought, is not on the seeker, then he is open territory. If you're unsure whether or not your friend is interested in the man, ask her. And if you know she is but hasn't been successful then let her know that you are also interested. You're not asking permission (no one owns him), but you are at least being out in the open. Although you can expect some friction to come out of this conversation, it is much better than going ahead without letting her know what your intentions are. It is very unfabulous to make a fool out of your friend because you're afraid of 'destroying her' when she finds out the man she pined for is actually mad for you. If, however, your friend is still in pursuit and it is unclear how the object of her attentions feels, then you absolutely may not make a move. Two friends battling it out over a man just gets silly. It can knock a solid friendship for six. And let's face it, no man is worth it.

Of course, if the man in question asks *you* out then you do not have to decline because you're worried about your friend's feelings. You may wish to probe first: 'I thought you and Fifi were getting close . . .' This will determine his interest, (and ensure he's not playing you both), and you can then come clean with Fifi.

THE AFFAIR – YOURS OR YOUR FRIEND'S, MALE OR FEMALE

Whether it's your illicit sex or your friend's, there are certain rules of decorum governing cheating hearts.

For one, you should not directly involve your friends in the romance. You may initially want to discuss your transgression in order to seek their advice, but if what you're really looking for is approval you may be disappointed. If a friend gives you a figurative slap in the face, you should respect that and, even if you do continue your affair, refrain from discussing it with this person.

Do not ask your friend to lie for you. As we've said, your moral compromise should not be foisted on another. Again, your FG friend may tell your husband you were with her once or twice, but she probably doesn't feel good about it.

This is also probably one of the only occasions where no introductions are necessary. Of course, being in the throes of passion with a new guy, you may be desperate to show off, perhaps even thinking that if your friend only met your lover she'd understand why you're cheating. Again, this is fooling yourself. It is best to remain discreet.

The wedding ring

A wise FG knows that she doesn't sleep with her lover in her marriage bed. But what of the ring? Does she whip it off every time she's with Mr Cheaterboy? The FG who is having the affair is obviously not respecting her husband, but somehow it is even worse to be getting it on in the back of the minivan while wearing the ring. Please remove it and place it in your bag.

The FG friend

As the innocent friend, it is up to you to decide how much of a moral high ground you want to take. In other situations, the Fabulous Girl knows how to confront the cheater urging the cheater to confess his or her crimes to the significant other (her friend) before the FG does. However, if it's the *cheater* who is your friend, then you have a more difficult choice.

Fine if you don't want to spill the beans. But do you publicly acknowledge this 'other' man or woman when you see him or her with your friend? Is your buddy hoping you'll offer your flat for 'lunch meetings'? Or that you'll include the lover in a dinner-party invitation? The FG will not snub the object of desire – just be polite and pretend it's your friend's friend. Like a colleague. You don't need to befriend the individual or spend hours with him or her at a country cottage on holidays, and you certainly shouldn't enable their affair by allowing them access to your spare room, but you shouldn't be rude to them either. After all, this is really your friend's business.

THE TWO-TIMER

There are certain types of men who decide to pursue two women at the same time. If such a man is really into living dangerously, he may attempt this with two women who know each other (or he may do so unwittingly, but he's still a two-timer). If the Fabulous Girl finds herself in this situation with another gal, she cannot be angry with *her*. It is bad behaviour *solely* on the male's part, and it is he who should feel her wrath. Actually, both their wraths. This is not a man who plays fair, and he really doesn't deserve any FG. In this case there is no need for competition, and if the other girl confronts the FG, the FG retorts, 'You can have him.'

WHEN NEW BOYS CHALLENGE FRIENDS

The Fabulous Girl enjoys visiting her friends, especially those that she doesn't see regularly. However, if her friend has a new boyfriend, the FG will naturally expect the dynamics to be altered. The three of them share dinner and a few bottles of Chablis, the FG thinks she's getting to know the new boyfriend and he seems cool. Then her pal passes out, drunk and tired. Suddenly New Boyfriend decides that this is the best moment to show the FG his erection and to confess that he's crazy about her and really wants to have sex. Naturally appalled, the Fabulous Girl declines and makes a hasty exit. The next morning she ponders what to do. Should she tell her friend about her lecherous beau? Her thoughts are interrupted by her telephone – it's her hungover friend calling to tell the FG to stay away from her boyfriend. Yes, apparently the rejected wannabe boy-toy beat the FG to the punch, only he reversed the facts, telling his girlfriend that the FG hit on *him*.

Unfortunately, when it comes to love, a girl may sometimes believe what she wants to and not the truth. The FG, of course, would tell the truth and remind her pal of their long friendship and how the FG has never lied before, compared to, say, the few months of the boyfriend's loyalty test. In most cases the woman will believe the FG.

137

If the FG is the girl with the loutish man, then she should consider the status of her friendship – how long, how honest, how much does she know her friend – contrasted with the knowledge of a recent boyfriend versus, say, a husband. And she should glean the truth.

SPECIAL LOVES

Many FGs have a man in their lives who plays an ambiguous role. Mostly a friendship, her attachment to this man was originally an erotic one. Maybe she met him and began a passionate affair with him while she was studying in Berlin. Perhaps they met in a queue for a film festival in New York. For some reason their affair never developed into a committed relationship, usually because of distance. But the FG thinks very fondly of this man and keeps in touch with him. When they find themselves in the same city, they often find themselves in the same bed. He is her special love. Although the FG and her special love have no formal commitment (the vague status of this relationship also means that it often has no end), it is understood by her friends that he is off limits to them. It doesn't matter if an FG's friend is going to be spending three weeks in Berlin and the special love has offered to show her around, the friend may not sleep with this man.

CHAPSTICKS

Your friend's ex

Chances are you've spent a good deal of time in the company of your best friend and her long-time beau. But if they split you may find yourself under pressure to cut him from your life. Your good pal may even ask you not to talk to her ex anymore. This is unreasonable, especially if you knew him prior to their relationship or if she was the one who left *him*. There is nothing wrong with the occasional drink or suchlike to stay in touch and to let him know that you're still his friend.

It is also rude to snub her ex at events or parties, even if the bastard broke your pal's heart. Only if he did something heinous to you personally or was abusive to your friend can you employ the FG snub tactic.

FG rule: Set limits on topics of conversation when in the ex's company – don't discuss your friend and their breakup in detail. He may need to vent if he's hurt, but he should not try to get you to diss your friend. Nor should he try to get you to give him advice on how to win her back or ask you to speak with her on his behalf. There is nothing more annoying for an FG than to have messages from her ex relayed through you: 'You know Bingo is really still in love with you, that night with Ethel meant nothing . . .'

FG off limits: Of course if you are engaging in lengthy phone chats or flirty e-mail exchanges with him, then your pal will rightly feel uncomfortable. She may even wonder if you're in hot pursuit of her ex. Perhaps you are. If so, you should come clean if you hope to maintain the friendship. You should allow some decent time to pass before pursuing the ex. But no matter how long a grace period you wait before beginning a romance with her ex, this new dating arrangement will make your pal feel awkward and perhaps hurt. You must be prepared for the possibility that your friendship will be altered for good.

We're just friends

An FG has male friends. She may even have very close friends who are men. This can be difficult for her boyfriend to accept. He may suspect that his FG is being at best naïve, at worst disingenuous, in insisting that her friendship with Mr Friendly is innocent. If it's at all possible, an FG should try to find a way of bringing her man and Mr Friendly together. Can they bond over their interest in Rohmer movies? Collect bottle caps together? If the FG can't quite put her finger on why she is uncomfortable with her boyfriend and her boy friend spending time together, she needs to take a closer look at these relationships. Do her feelings for Mr Friendly run a little deeper than she's confessing? Is she protecting Mr Friendly because she knows he's secretly in love with her? In fact, an overuse of the very phrase, 'We're just friends' implies that you are worried about it being otherwise.

Not your normal fuck buddy: How to keep a friendship after sex

You and Bingo have known each other forever. He's always been such a great friend. Then it happened. Too many glasses of wine, a bad breakup – any number of things could have led you down the garden path with a pal. At first it seemed like such a good idea. You like each other so much, why not just take the next step? But as the sun rises, things look a little different. You look at each other and one of you regrets it and there's no denying it. Either things didn't go as smoothly as they might have or you just know in the light of day that your relationship is never going to make the transition to romance.

The main thing is to not overreact. Get up, make breakfast, or better yet, go out for breakfast. A change of scenery will make you both more comfortable. You've been to cafés together before and it's always been just fine, right? Someone does have to say something about this eventually, so the FG should be the bigger person and take the initiative. It may be that all you have to say is 'I really hope that what happened the other night isn't going to jeopardize our friendship. How are you feeling about it?' If you suspect that he would like this incident to ring a shift away from friendship toward romance, then you are especially obliged to speak up right away. Don't make him squirm wondering how you feel.

I don't always agree with Missy's tactics.
She can be a bit brash, but every once in a while she has a
point. It was this whole pregnancy of Eleanor's. We loved
Eleanor, but we also thought that being a single mum
wouldn't be as easy as she was making out. Missy had
decided that we couldn't just sit by and watch our best
friend's life spiral out of control. She convinced me to stick
my nose in and talk to Bingo.

'Just find out how he feels about Eleanor. You don't have
to tell him about the baby.'

'But what if he's not the father?'

'What does that matter as long as he's a good provider?'
Missy could be very calculating. 'If he still loves her, maybe
that would be good.'

Begrudgingly, I agreed to call Bingo. Missy never could
stomach the man, and I knew that if she were to call him
he'd be very suspicious. He didn't seem that surprised
when I asked him to meet me for coffee. He suggested
cocktails, and not wanting to make him wonder about our
upcoming conversation, I agreed.

I waited for him for forty-five minutes, drinking a glass of
champagne. I was glad that I had suggested my favourite
hotel bar. It was a large room, but it had many private
nooks for intimate conversation. I figured that if our little
talk went well – I pictured Bingo breaking down and

admitting his faults, confessing his love for Eleanor and his hope that she'd come back to him so that they could settle down – he would be glad not to have an obvious audience witnessing his tears. To that end, I had chosen a sofa for two in a dark corner. I sat and sipped for another full fifteen minutes. Finally, the man of the hour showed up, in scruffy jeans and a corduroy blazer. What did Eleanor see in him?

'This is a pleasant surprise.' He tried to kiss me on the lips. I averted my head, and his lips landed somewhere between my earlobe and my collar.

The champagne had made me brave, hopefully brave enough, so I decided to dive right in to the business at hand. 'Actually, I have something to ask you.'

Bingo leaned in. He reeked of rum. 'Not before I get a drink. Hey, can I get some service here?'

With every passing second I was reminded of why I disliked Bingo. I began to silently wish that the stranger in the gents' was the baby's father.

'Bingo, how do you feel about Eleanor?'

'I haven't felt Eleanor in months!' He roared at his own pathetic humour.

I tried to stay on course, 'Are you saying you don't care about her anymore? You're in love with Mel?'

'She dumped me.'

'Eleanor?'

'Mel. Nay, my Eleanor rocks.'

Hmm. This was a sign of sorts. Maybe he did love her, maybe his bad clothes and foul breath were all because he was pining for Eleanor.

'I've been doing this nineteen-year-old since Mel,' Bingo winked. 'Much fresher.'

That did it – I was totally repulsed. I didn't want Bingo to know about the baby, his or not. Of course Eleanor knew what she was doing; she'd do just fine with the kind of support she'd have. Missy and I would be good aunts. It would be a piece of cake. I started to get up from the sofa. 'Look at the time – I have a date with Nice.'

Bingo grabbed my arm.

'Don't go, I've always liked the looks of you, kiddo.' He pulled me down onto his lap and stuck his hand up my skirt, pawing at my thigh. Now, I'd never hit a person before, but suddenly my inner Bette Davis awakened and whammo! Well, if you want to silence a room, slapping a man across the face is a surefire conversation ender.

'Do not ever come near me or Eleanor again.' I raised my voice for added drama, since all eyes were on me anyway. At least people would know my violent outburst was justified.

Looking straight ahead, I marched out of the room, catching Dudley at the bar on my way out. Had he witnessed my little performance? Who was I kidding – the bastard was taking notes. Once outside, I slumped against the wall. Why did I ever listen to Missy?

The next thing I did was to tell Eleanor everything. Well, that was the second thing – my first call was to Missy. She needed to be on the other side of my rant and rage. I insisted we spill all to Eleanor, before she read about it and thought *I* was sleeping with Bingo.

Naturally, Eleanor was furious. For a brief second I think she did suspect that I had a thing for her ex. Luckily Missy was added proof to the contrary. I couldn't blame Eleanor for her anger – she was at least relieved that I hadn't mentioned the baby to him. Almost too relieved.

'Bingo is not the father.'

Missy and I were silent.

'It was that guy. My baby was conceived in a toilet,'

144

Eleanor was getting upset, that lethal combo of hormones and bad memories. 'I can't even remember what he looked like.'

Trouble was, neither could I. I hadn't seen him before or since. Eleanor was truly on her own.

CHAPTER FIVE

*Sex and
Courtship*

Dudley had a field day with the Bingo
incident. The section editor at the paper was all over me to
fight back, to fight back as Manners Girl. Bradley still didn't
care what I did as long as my *Smack!* work didn't suffer.
So I battled it out with Dudley for two weeks. I tried to
convey that, while I did not condone violence in any way,
there was a certain appeal to the centuries-old reaction of
striking someone with a proverbial glove. That duels have a
place, and that communicating one's displeasure or defend-
ing one's honour is an integral part of keeping society on its
best-behaved toes. That we often let people get away with
terrible acts out of fear of being disliked or being politically
incorrect. But I added a caution: such extreme behaviour
should not be tried at home.

Readers wrote both in my defence and in denouncement,
but the controversy sold like hotcakes, so the newspaper
was happy. The section editor seemed to indicate that he
wanted more regular stuff from me, but he wouldn't
commit. In fact, I was lucky on two counts: Bingo wasn't
going to charge me with assault. Apparently he had a criminal record for drunk driving and didn't want to mess with
the cops, so he decided to take it like a man and refused to
discuss it. In fact, it made him seem more glamorous to that
certain type of woman who worshipped 'bad boys,' and he
got lots of female attention.

* * *

Glowing in my minor notoriety, we all attended a party shortly after my altercation with Bingo. Despite the hoopla, or perhaps because of it, our group dynamic was out of whack. Nice was behaving oddly, Missy was still without Joe (in fact, it had been months since I'd seen him with her) and Eleanor was adjusting to being a party girl without alcohol.

Nice had brought along Francis, a new colleague from the investment firm he worked for. Francis and Missy were chatting up a storm. I tried to flirt with Nice, but his face was serious, as if something was on his mind. Meanwhile, Eleanor had picked up a handsome guy named Josh.

At the end of the evening she whispered in my ear, 'I'm leaving with Josh. He's going to drive me home.' They took off. I thought nothing of it since (a) Eleanor wasn't drunk and (b) she was pregnant.

'Let's go to my place,' I cooed to Nice.

'I think I may pass tonight.'

'Not feeling well?' I offered. Who was this guy, and where was Nice?

'Yeah, I'm sick.'

Sighing, I looked around for Missy, but she was nowhere to be seen.

'We should say goodnight to Missy and Francis.'

'I don't think we should disturb them.' Nice pointed toward a small collection of potted plants. Sandwiched between a palm and a fig tree were Missy and Francis, necking.

'What do I do now?'

'Go home. She's a grown-up, you know. You can't spend your whole life meddling.'

Nice wasn't being very nice. I didn't see what he was getting at. In fact, all I did get was a goodnight kiss in the cab and my empty loft. Kitty, at least, was happy to see me.

I tossed and turned all night. It was lonely without Nice. Lonelier not knowing why he was being so not Nice.

The next morning, around eight-thirty, my phone rang. I was barely awake – it was, after all, a Sunday. It had to be Nice.

It was Eleanor.

'I hate men.'

'You're pregnant. Of course you do.'

'That Josh, he's one of the worst.'

'Why, what happened?'

'I need breakfast. Can I come over?'

I scrambled some eggs for the two of us, still wondering why Nice hadn't called.

Eleanor sat down and shovelled the food in like she was never going to eat again. Between mouthfuls she told me about the events after the party. Josh had indeed driven her home, and she had invited him up. They really connected. One thing led to another, and they had sex. The sex was great. Afterwards he was loving and cuddly, and wanted to stay over. Things were just fine until around seven, when she woke up with severe morning sickness.

'I spent ten minutes puking, it was awful. Josh was all concerned, asked me if I had a hangover. I told him, "No, you idiot, I'm pregnant."'

'Pregnant? I thought you were just voluptuous.'

Apparently Josh hadn't taken the news very well. He'd freaked out and fled from her place barely dressed.

'What a bastard,' spat Eleanor.

'But Eleanor, why didn't you tell him? I mean, being pregnant is a pretty big deal.'

'It was none of his business.' She did have a point. Still, it would be quite a shock to discover that the stranger you'd just slept with was pregnant. Eleanor never heard from Josh again.

Sex & Courtship

The Fabulous Girl's Life wouldn't be fulfilled without great sex, being courted by handsome men and the discovery of love with the one of her choice. Sigh. However, all three of these necessities have their ups and downs and the FG must learn to tread lightly on egos, say no to bad situations and keep the fire in her relationship – sometimes all at the same time! While this may sound exhausting the Fabulous Girl is never too tired to pursue a fine romance.

Sex, Sex, Sex

Booty calls

It's late on a Thursday night, you're home alone and you're feeling a certain, shall we say, restlessness? What's an FG to do? Rather than ordering pizza, you pick up the phone for another kind of delivery. That dial-a-date call that's really not about a date at all. In fact, you're not going to be leaving your apartment. That's right, just recreational sex, no strings attached. There are FGs who have the booty call down to such a science they've coined a code phrase 'Are you free for Cosmopolitans tonight?' It's perfectly acceptable to invite someone over for sex, but the Fabulous Girl gets some graciously.

Who do you love?

You can only make a booty call when you are single. No exceptions, ever. And you can only make booty calls to other single people. We don't want to hear about it otherwise. Top of the list are those casual lovers with whom you've become friendly but not relationshippy. You must be careful that your booty call is not toying with the affections of a vulnerable man. Some guy you kind of like but whom you know to be in love with you should not be on the receiving end – in other words, no platonic Chapsticks. The best bet for booty is an ex-lover or a one-night stand from the past – your fuck-buddy Chapstick. The ex-lover must not be a newly minted breakup boy, but after a year or two go ahead and dial him up. You cannot underestimate the comfort of a familiar boudoir partner.

Cosmos?

Be clear what it is you're after. Men often think they have to lay on the romance to get sex, but this will only confuse the matter if what you want is just to get physical. If you make your position clear from the beginning, you will save yourself the awkward 'But what did it mean?' conversation the next day.

Setting the scene

FGs know that even a booty call requires some ambience. Lay on the candles, wine, music and freshly fluffed pillows. Just because it's only sex, there's no reason not to do it right. And if the FG is heading out for booty, while she doesn't need to show up in a corset (unless she wants to), she does at the very least need to shower! Bringing a bottle of bubbly is also decorous.

Once there

Pour the vino, sit down and let the flirtations begin. And do take the time to make some conversation.

Thanks for having me!

Even if the booty calls get to be a regular thing, or even if it's the first time, the Fabulous Girl always rings the next day to say thank you – particularly if she was the one who made the booty call.

BOY BENDERS

A Fabulous Girl knows that she can have sex as often and with as many boys as she wants. It may be that she's out of university and is stretching her wings in a new town, or maybe she's recently finished with a long-term relationship. Either way, when the FG wants it, she gets it. But sometimes it's a case of so many men, so little time, because choosing partners for a boy bender is much less fraught than looking for a mate. He needs to be single, and really sexy. And since there are so many sexy ones out there, why choose only one?

There are, however, certain protocols for managing a boy bender, as it's only a boy bender if there's more than one involved.

First of all, the sex is casual. You may have amazing in-depth discussions about Shakespeare or the plight of the rainforest, but the sex is just sex. If you start to fantasize about him being your boyfriend or you get possessive when you see him flirting with another at a party, you are no longer on a boy bender.

Booty calls are appropriate during boy benders. All you need to do is ask and they will come. You need to say thank you the next day, but you owe nothing more.

If your boys overlap, it is a good idea to select them from different social groups. While the notion of a bad reputation may seem outdated, it is wiser to keep your lovers out of the same gossip loop. You don't want one of them to mention to the other the hot night he spent with his babe. An FG doesn't enjoy seeing two men fight over her. Okay, maybe just a little. It also helps if one boy is in your city and the other is a long-distance romance. That's right, boy benders can still be infused with romance, just not commitment.

There is no need to answer prying questions from the men. 'Are you seeing anyone else?' should be dealt with by a swift, 'I see people.' But leave it at that. He doesn't really want to hear about how sexy that Italian actor in Manchester is. And you probably don't want to learn of his bombshell from Bristol either. But you should be clear about being on a bender so no one gets their feelings hurt.

KISSING & TELLING

Everyone knows that women talk to each other about sex more than men do. Men live in fear of this fact, and with good reason. Girlfriends have no compunction about sharing the intimate details of their current and past affairs. However, there are limits to how much you should shag and tell.

'Was he good?'

You can only answer this in the affirmative. The only man who may be dissed on skill is a lout, an out-of-towner or someone no one in your social group will ever see again. It's very badly played to sleep with someone all your friends know and then spend a girls-only dinner party detailing the ways that he let you down in bed. The worst thing you can allow yourself to confess is 'We didn't click.'

Size matters

To men. So unless you're telling war stories from back in the day, refrain from getting into issues of length and girth. Some cheeky friends may ask you outright if your new lover is a well-hung stud. A polite FG should answer simply, 'Everybody is very happy.'

155

Disease

You never have the right to disclose details of someone else's health issues.

'He does this thing'

It's perfectly acceptable to describe technique to other FGs without disclosing names. This is simply doing your part for the sisterhood. 'I had a boyfriend once who could do the most amazing things with his hips. Have you and Alfred tried it with your legs inside his?'

SEX ON THE SPOT

Got to have it right now? No, not that great pair of Jimmy Choos, but S-E-X. You and your boyfriend have been getting way too hot and heavy walking around the gallery and it's far too long a cab ride back to your place. The Fabulous Girl knows that sex in public isn't necessarily proper but sometimes she just can't help herself. The FG does, however, know a few good rules for sexy conduct away from the bedroom:

1. *Don't* assume that if you can't see them, they can't see you. Any couple canoodling in the back seat of a car may have an audience. People love being voyeurs, so know that you are taking the risk of being watched. But then that is no doubt part of the excitement, isn't it? And yes, the car will rock and the windows will fog, so they know what's happening even when they can't see you.

2. *Don't* choose places where the physical discomfort outweighs the thrill. Avoid rocky beaches (*sans* blanket), and, despite the reputation, airplane loos are too tiny and smelly. However, as one Fabulous Girl discovered, the wacky theme hotels in Vegas often have many nooks, crannies and fountains to help camouflage your little party (especially at night).

3. *Don't* involve people around you. If you are one of those people who wants to make out at the movies, make it a matinee where the crowd will be sparse and you can plant yourselves well away from others. Never start anything when people are close enough to you to be made uncomfortable or to have their movie viewing disturbed.

4. *Don't* take all day. If you are making it in a toilet where people have the expectation of a short wait, make it snappy.

5. *Do* keep the noise down. Loud moaning or shouting your lover's name will only draw attention to your activity, and could get you arrested.

6. *Do* know your lover's comfort level. If showing up at his office wearing only a trench coat will mortify him, don't force the issue.

7. *Do* leave nothing behind but footprints.

PHONE SEX

It's what those old long-distance commercials really meant about that long-distance feeling. If you are separated from your lover or just too lazy to get in a cab over to his place late at night, phone sex is a surprisingly good substitute for the real thing. Those who are new to phone sex may feel a little silly at first. It is only sexy if both of you are into it. And it is quite rude to be talking dirty while ironing or watching a gardening show on television. If you are, then you are not having phone sex, you are a phone sex worker. If you're not in the mood for it, your partner will know and it just won't work.

The optimal time for phone sex is late at night before drifting off to sleep, not during your office lunch break (too many distractions). Your lover may ask you to describe in detail things that your mother would scream if she heard. Do it anyway. Phone sex has to be totally reciprocal to be successful –

this means expressing your fantasies as well as playing out his. One of the real benefits of phone sex is that inhibitions fall away when no one is watching. It makes for good practice for later when you are together. Once success has been reached you cannot hang up immediately or answer the call waiting – it is time for phone-line pillow talk.

GETTING WHAT YOU WANT

It's one of the most painful yet prevalent myths that if you really like someone, you'll have great sex. Oh, would it were true. But as every FG knows, having conversational or intellectual chemistry with someone does not necessarily mean your click will be heard in the bedroom. Still, it is possible to get what you want out of sex.

The confident Fabulous Girl understands that a spoonful of sugar really does make the medicine go down. Try a little inventive encouragement before anything else. Telling a man he has great hands will induce him to use them, and from there the FG can do the guiding.

Of course, some men need less subtle hints. If the compliment route doesn't get you there, you'll have to be more direct. Don't be shy. Forget the idea that it's not sexy to ask for what you want in bed. It would be rude not to give your lover the chance to rock your world just because you didn't want to speak up.

Tit for tat

The FG fancies herself good in bed, and part of maintaining that is knowing what her lover wants. So even if you despise having your ear kissed, indulge him; it's likely a sign he'd like the manoeuvre reciprocated. Likewise, if you swoon when you ankles are stroked, make a play for his; a sensitive lover will get the message that you'd like some ankle action yourself. But it's not necessary that lovemaking be exactly reciprocal. Sex would be rather dull if it were simply a ping-pong game of I-do-it-to-you-and-then-you-do-it-to-me. There is, of course, a comfort-level issue too: if you really get squeamish about a specific thing, then you should just say so.

Conversation

Talk is not cheap in bed. Conventional wisdom says you shouldn't engage in potentially difficult conversations about sex while you're in bed. Pshaw. Where are you going to have those little chats, in aisle 4 of Sainsburys? We're not recommending a talk that takes place during lovemaking, rather some other quiet time in bed, say, Sunday morning. However, if you are in the throes of passion, there is no better time to whisper seductive instructions to him. In this case, it may be wiser to show than to tell.

Being a great lover, the FG also understands that it is better to give. The flip side of all this advice is generosity. Going out of your way to please a lover is not only polite, it ups the likelihood that he'll do the same for you.

AND THERE IT GOES

You think everything is going swimmingly, and then suddenly it's not and then he rolls off of you and stares up at the ceiling. He's lost his hard-on and in its place a black cloud is hovering over the bed. It happens. No man likes it, and few handle the situation well. The main thing is to keep things light – at least on your part. Ask him if he'd like you to . . . or maybe he'd like it if you gave him a little . . . or would he like to take a break for a couple of minutes? Whatever you do, don't prop up on on one elbow, look searchingly in his eyes and ask, 'What's wrong?' The word 'wrong' spoken in the vicinity of a flaccid penis has very bad juju for men. Don't do it. And though you may be frustrated that things have ground to a halt, it's better to change the subject and talk about something else, maybe mention that you're quite tired yourself. Although you may be thinking. 'Well, it doesn't stop me from being able to have an orgasm!' it's probably best to just let that slide this time.

I LOVE YOU, YOU LOVE ME NOT

A surefire passion killer is confessing your love for a new beau only to have him go cold or simply pretend he didn't hear you. How do you handle it when you say 'I love you' first and he doesn't respond in kind? It's a nightmare, basically. A good guy will try to make you feel okay about this situation even if he's not ready to speak the words you were hoping for. He'll tell you how happy that makes him and how much you mean to him. If he freezes or looks terrified, you're with a man with little grace. A man with little grace who doesn't love you. Get out.

VD TALK

The time to discuss health issues with a new lover is before sex. It's a given that you're going to be using condoms when you start a new romance. But what if there's something particular for you to say? For example, 'I have herpes'? You cannot in good conscience start a romance without being honest about the state of your health. You must give the new lover the chance to make a choice, and you must tell him about it before you have sex. The information needn't be dispensed on your first introduction – wait until you know that sex is a given in every other way. Maybe there's been some snogging on the couch and he asks if you can move the action into the bedroom. That's your moment. While you're still comfortably wrapped up, calmly tell him there's something he needs to know.

That is, of course, if your sexually transmitted disease is a permanent one. If what you have is something such as chlamydia, which can be successfully treated, then you don't have to tell him. Unfortunately, many people consider VD a dirty, despicable thing that only the sexually promiscuous can catch. They're wrong, but the stigma survives. But while you can protect your privacy, you *can't* have sex with him – not even with a condom. Just be patient until you get your negative test result and then you can have all the fun you want.

If you are given this kind of information by a new lover, it behooves you to receive the news with grace. You must be warm and non-judgmental about it even if what you decide is to end the courtship.

Breaking it to your mate that you have VD

There's no easy way to break the news to your boyfriend that you have a sexually transmitted disease. Especially since the implication is so obvious it glows in the dark – you cheated on him. In fact, it may be better to tell him first about your indiscretion, then admit that the story doesn't end with the affair. What happens to your relationship will be up to the two of you. You cannot mess with his health.

Honey, you gave me warts!

If you are in a long-term relationship and you've recently found suspicious bumps down there, you will probably be shocked and angered by your discovery. But if your lover is denying any wrong-doing, he may just be innocent. Learn the facts. If it's something such as warts or herpes, then it could have been dormant and only just surfaced. However, you have the right to be upset for not having been warned about the risk involved in even a dormant virus. This is a vitally important trust issue. Of course, if it isn't something that recurs, you may have a cheater on your hands. Unlike with a new lover, there is no need to behave with stoicism. Feel free to be angry. Feel free to storm out of the room. Feel free to dump him.

Telling an ex-lover you may have given him VD
If you only recently discovered your 'problem' and you're single, you have a different set of dilemmas on your hands. You realize that it could have been one of five men who gave it to you, and that means you may have given it to any and all of the others. Ugh. You need to tell everyone what's going on. This needn't be a long call, but a simple 'You should know . . . I'm sorry.' In fact, some STD clinics will do this for you. You give them the list, they'll place the calls without giving your name. The seriousness of the disease may determine how you handle the situation.

UNEXPECTED PREGNANCIES

No matter how super extra strength the condom she employed along with her birth control pill was, sometimes a woman gets pregnant without planning on it. If this happens, she does need to tell the man involved. This should be done in person and in private. No beating around the bush either. Just say it like it is.

Unfortunately, there are men out there who will doubt that they are the father of the child. Some cads may deny responsibility until provided with proof. It is sad but true that you may have to get DNA evidence to confirm what you already know to be true.

A certain famous Fabulous Girl was publicly humiliated

when her boyfriend denied his responsibility for her pregnancy. Of course, she handled it with her trademark sophistication and did not resort to hysterics or mudslinging. And in the end, her quiet confidence prevailed when it was proven that the lout was the father.

Now, FGs are sexually liberated, so if you've been on a boy bender and find yourself with child but without secure knowledge of the father's identity, then you need to inform the boys that fatherhood is pending for one of them. This may seem unreasonable or unfair for the FG, but it is not only her life at stake; the child and man have to be thought of too.

In all of these cases, an FG needs to think carefully about how she will manage her future. And her baby's future. Although she may be able to extract financial assistance from the father, it is not possible to extract a partnership from a man who was made a parent against his will.

Courtship

WHEN BAD DATES HAPPEN TO GOOD FGS

Sex without love can be fine for the single FG. But if a relationship is what she's after, then she must enter the dating minefield. The truth of the matter is that no one really enjoys dating. Dating is a horrid ritual designed to weed out the unwanted and the undesirable. Of course, it may take years of marriage to truly know whether one made the right choice, but often one or two dates (or one or two minutes) may suffice.

Making a break for it

Date going badly? He's a total jerk? The Fabulous Girl knows the difference between a dull man – she simply declines dessert and coffee and goes home – and the asshole who spends dinner ranting about what bitches all his exes (and women in general) are. If it's the latter, the FG can make a guilt-free run for it. A sudden headache, a forgotten meeting, an unexpected business trip with an early morning flight all are acceptable excuses. However, heading to the ladies only never to return is not okay. If the man is truly offensive, there is nothing wrong with the FG's speaking her mind: 'You know, Bob, I think you're just too angry towards brunettes and your language is too offensive for me to want to continue our date. Thanks for dinner.' With this and a toss of her hair, the FG can leave. If you don't care for the notion of owing this lout anything, then toss a twenty on the table as you flounce out the door.

Oops, did I forget to mention I have a boyfriend?

Perhaps it's a professional circumstance that has brought you and the Handsome Stranger into such close quarters. You exchange casual banter at first, not thinking much about the situation – you'll probably never see the guy again, right? Then your chat turns serious, you start riffling on art, literature, cinema, you're really hitting it off. This is fun. Until at the end it seems that your Handsome Stranger now has a crush on *you*. But your boyfriend never came up. Why would he, considering that the intention of the meeting was business – who could have predicted such a spontaneous connection? Besides, this innocent flirting is fun. Why ruin it with a bit of fact?

Trouble is, Handsome has now invited you out for lunch to discuss things further. Ugh. The nagging question is this: Has he asked you out? Or is he just being friendly?

When does an FG admit to having a full-time boyfriend? No one should introduce themselves to a member of the opposite sex by saying, 'Hi, I'm FG and I have a boyfriend.'

Likewise, if Handsome does invite you to his home for a dinner party with a select number of people, how can you be sure that he doesn't simply think you're a fascinating person (which as an FG you are)? If you say, 'I'd love to come, but you have to know I have a boyfriend,' it can only lead to the embarrassing response, 'That's fine, I'm not really interested in you in *that* way.' Mortifying.

If, dear FG, you find yourself asked on some sort of quasi-date, you should simply decline. But do not use your beau as the excuse. Rather next time you speak to Handsome, let it drop: 'My boyfriend and I are heading to Paris for the week-end, I *so* need a holiday . . .' Or if there's an event where Handsome will be, bring your beau along and introduce them. Another last resort in desperate times is to have a mutual friend let Handsome know the truth. This can actually spare both of you the awkwardness.

YOUR CRUSH

He's handsome, smart and witty and has a dynamic career. So now you have a crush. He's also single. Your crush just got worse. You want to date him, sleep with him, fall in love and marry him. Trouble is, he doesn't seem to know you're alive. But what is even more mortifying is that despite your FG-ness, every time he comes your way to talk to you (he seems interested), you babble like a fool. Your jokes aren't funny. You stutter. The best plan of action in this case is to shut up. Do less and don't try to impress until your nervousness wears off. Your reticence will draw him to you. At least this way you'll seem mysterious not goofy.

While crushes can be crushing, there is no reason that an FG has to sit on the sidelines when he's around. If he still doesn't get how fab you are, then allow the FG in you to take over and ask him out. That's right, this is where those art

165

gallery tickets you just happened to have will come in handy. And since you've traded in your nervous Nelly-when-he's around self for the cool air of aloofness, if he does turn you down, it won't show.

MATCH-MAKING FGS

So your friend Sophie is fabulous and single, and your Chapstick Harrison is amazing and surprisingly single. What's an FG to do? She wants everyone to be happy and find love, or at least great sex, so she sets them up. Only Sophie is still reeling from a breakup and Harrison just wants to have fun, so their date is a disaster. Sophie talks endlessly about her doomed affair with Bingo, and Harrison can't stop flirting with the pretty waitress. This type of incident could have been avoided if FG had done her research. It is highly unfabulous to set up two people who are not in the same mental place, no matter how good you think they'd be together or how much you think they have in common.

Sometimes a person will agree to be set up without actually being ready. They'll feel pressured to get back into the dating game when really what they need is time alone. Often friends don't understand this need and keep nagging their single friend to 'Get out there.' Wherever 'there' is exactly isn't clear. It is far better to tell your friend that you know of another singleton when she's ready to date.

If the Fabulous Girl is the one being forced into set-ups, she should remember she never has to cave to these pressures. A firm 'I'm not ready, but thanks for thinking of me,' is enough.

Let's face it, most set-ups don't work. There's something inherently unromantic about them. One Fabulous Girl went hopefully to a friend's potluck to be set up; unfortunately, the intended man sat opposite her eating potato salad with his hands. An FG always favours the fantasy of meeting that sexy stranger on her own, where the two of them just can't take their eyes off each other. But if she's game then at least she can discover for herself if being set up is for her.

BLIND DATES

In some cultures, blind dates are the standard mode of meeting potential mates. In others, it's hell in a bread basket. If you decide to embark on a date with a man you've never met – or worse, never even seen a photo of – then be prepared to run.

Agree to meet only in a public place. Arrange for afternoon coffee so that you can escape as soon as possible if necessary. In fact, if you see him and know immediately that the thought of him laying a hand on you is grounds for antacid then order a cold beverage, such as iced tea, that you can down in a hurry.

Dress nicely for your meeting, but not too sexy, just in case you have the above-mentioned reaction. You are also never obliged to give out your home number or address, or to agree to another date if you don't want to. If the blind date came through a friend, then you are probably less concerned about him being a mad killer, but if you got him through the personals, on- or off-line, then be cautious. In the latter situation you can even drag a friend along to sit anonymously at another table and keep her eye on things.

Always bring your mobile with you on dates. That way you can nip to the ladies' room and make a quick call to a friend to discuss how things are going or ask for advice. Or ask her and her boyfriend to meet you at a bar in half an hour so you can have a change of scenery.

SAYING NO TO THE SECOND DATE

If you went out on a first date with a man, it's likely that he will want to go on a second date with you. But if things didn't really go well on the first, the FG will have a hard time gearing up for another try. Being an instinctive, passionate girl, this just isn't likely. You owe it to the guy to let him know the truth right away. Not that you never want to see him naked – although that's obviously true. That you're not going to go out again. Tell him you're not ready to date right now. Tell him you don't think the two of you made that kind of connection. Whatever you do, don't sound overly apologetic. This is and will be perceived as patronizing. Avoid the really bad clichés – I'd like to be friends, you're a great guy. You shouldn't imagine that he doesn't already know that.

The Men

For the Fabulous Girl heading toward thirty, the men who are available to court her may shift in demographic. The single ones may be single for a reason, divorced or much younger than she. These men represent the extreme ends of the single-guy spectrum and come with their own warning labels.

DIVORCING MAN

This is a man in transition. He's both vulnerable and bitter. The first may appeal to the FG, but the second will drive her nuts. This period will include long, intimate and tearful conversations with the estranged wife and perhaps their kids.

Danger Zone: He's going to be sad. He's going to be angry. He's going to use you as his rebound.

Early Warning Signs: He won't stop talking about the divorce, the legal fees and how he wishes it had all worked out differently.

THE SECOND-HAND MAN

Stage two of the above. However, he's probably had his rebound. In some ways these men make the best potential partners. They've been through a marriage, so chances are their expectations are more realistic. In this situation the Fabulous Girl will shine. But if he's paying alimony or child support, the FG needs to be aware that his financial – and in the case of kids, emotional – priorities may lie elsewhere.

Danger Zone: Bitterness may still linger, depending on the divorce.

Early Warning Signs: Every time you have an argument, he compares you to his ex-wife.

MR DAD

The older you get – or the older your dates get – the more likely it is that each of you will be bringing more than psychological baggage to the new relationship. You may meet a man who not only has been married in the past but has kids.

If you're dating someone with kids, it's wise to put off meeting them until you and your man are very certain that this is going to be a long-term relationship. It's too hard on you and it's not fair to them otherwise. Make this clear to your new guy right from the start. Let him know that you appreciate how important his children are to him. In fact, that's exactly why you'd rather wait to meet them, because you recognize that their well-being should be treated seriously. And really, you owe it to yourself to see how serious you are about him before you wade into what will certainly be a difficult situation.

Danger Zone: She needs to decide if she can play second fiddle to the kids, or at least feel non-competitive.

Early Warning Signs: He constantly cancels plans to be with the kids but you're never invited to join in.

OLDER MAN

Some FGs swear by older men: they tend to appreciate the FGs wit, passion and – okay, let's say it – her youthful skin and body. It would be unrealistic to say that the older guy doesn't on some level relish the simple fact that the FG is younger, but that shouldn't be the sole reason to be together. The Fabulous Girl will appreciate the older guy who has already accomplished many of his professional goals, who is happy with who he is and where he is at this stage of his life. This type of solid man can be a great support to the FG who is still working on her career. Sex with the older guy can also be great, he probably knows a few things the FG doesn't, yet he's patient enough to take time with sex. But be aware that women of *his* generation will often resent you and give you dirty looks – even in the supermarket.

Danger Zone: The FG may be a mere trophy girl.

Early Warning Signs: Your intimate dinner dates are few. Instead, he always takes you to cocktail parties and business functions where he can show you off.

170

YOUNGER MAN

The main benefit to the Fabulous Girl here is sex, sex and sex. The college-age student may not appeal to the FG for long, but his admiration for his 'older' lover and his libido are a great distraction in-between more serious relationships.

Danger Zone: In the majority of cases, he is a mere dalliance.

Early Warning Signs: His age.

DIFFERENT MAN

If the Fabulous Girl is trying to change her 'type,' she may find herself in unfamiliar waters. If the dark, brooding sculptor is the one who makes her melt but breaks her heart, the FG may wish to go the opposite direction and date a highly rational lawyer or scientist. For this huge swing, the FG must be open-minded and patient, not just dismiss the guy on the first date because he doesn't mould clay with his bare hands. She needs to uncover what other types of chemistry may be brought out.

Danger Zone: You may have a type for a reason, and the different man will not be challenging and engaging in the ways that matter to the FG.

Early Warning Signs: You keep telling your friends that he's great, but you can't understand why you're not more attracted to him.

Rich man

Many women target a Mr Rich. The Fabulous Girl cannot deny the pleasure of the finer things in life. If she gets involved with a rich man, however, she may find that he not only pays for everything, he makes all the decisions too. Where you eat, what play you see, where you holiday. It is up to the FG to decide her threshold for passivity.

Danger Zone: You get too used to the fine life but can't afford it without Mr Rich.

Early Warning Signs: You stop even reaching for the cheque.

Poor man

Depending on the financial status of the FG, dating a man of little economic means will resonate differently. If both of you are poor, then there may be no tension around money. But if the Fabulous Girl has some money and has fallen for a starving actor, she may end up supporting them in a lifestyle only she can afford.

Danger Zone: It is easy for this situation to turn from romance to resentment – on both sides.

Early Warning Signs: He says no to your invitations to dine out.

CHEAP MAN

This one is easy for the Fabulous Girl. Get rid of him. There is nothing less attractive than a cheap man. Every single thing you want to do as a couple will be fraught. He will nix your choice of clothing, cars, décor, art. He seems to be saving for a rainy day that never comes.

Danger Zone: You'll convince yourself that he's just good with money.

Early Warning Signs: He asks you out on a first date and all you order is a cranberry juice, but he doesn't offer to pay and instead splits the bill.

THE CONTROL FREAK

Everything you do has to be done his way. Right down to how you slice bread. It takes a very strong FG to put up with this crap. She's going to have to tell him where to put his 'advice' until he learns to back off.

Danger Zone: You may start to doubt yourself and lose confidence.

Early Warning Signs: He starts most sentences with a version of 'That's not how you do it . . .'

BAD IN BED

No matter how much encouragement an FG gives to a new lover, there are times when the sexual chemistry just isn't there. And the sad fact is, it never will be there. If the sex is still bad after five months, it won't get better. This is cause enough to end the relationship. Those who say sex isn't that important have never had great sex.

Danger Zone: You convince yourself that he's perfect in every other way.

Early Warning Signs: See Danger Zone.

Eleanor seemed to be accepting that being pregnant was going to alter her dating habits until the baby was born. One friend's drama solved. And what about Nice? He was still behaving strangely. He was distant yet refused to discuss it. Then there was Missy. She invited me over for dinner, sent the car and driver for me and everything. Joe was away on business.

'I want to have an affair with Francis.'

'I did notice you kissing him at that party.' I was trying to be calm but I was wondering if all my friends had lost their minds. 'Did you sleep together?'

'Not yet.'

Of course, I wanted to ask why she wanted to have an affair, but it was usually better to let Missy ask the questions.

'What do you think?'

'I think you're married, Missy.'

She sighed. This clearly wasn't the response she wanted.

Then she talked and talked and talked. How Joe didn't seem to love her, how he was just an idiot who couldn't rake leaves properly let alone have sex with any degree of passion. He was always working and just wasn't fun any-more. She wanted a divorce.

Missy had gotten married in a hurry, so if her marriage

didn't work it wasn't exactly a shock to me. Joe was nice, but in a vacant sort of way. None of us, Missy included, really seemed to know what he did. Still, I couldn't lie.

'But Missy, it's your marriage. Don't you owe it to Joe and yourself to try harder?'

'Ugh, what do you know?' she snapped at me.

'I know that fucking Francis isn't going to make your marriage better. And that if what you want is a divorce then you should leave Joe and forget about the affair thing. It's not you.'

I could tell Missy wasn't pleased. She'd enjoyed that exciting first-kiss rush she'd had with Francis. The rush which married people obsess over losing and which gives single people no small amount of anxiety.

'If you have an affair you'll regret it. What if Francis *is* the right guy?'

Missy was piqued.

'If Francis is the *one*, do you want to begin the relationship full of lies and deceit? He'd never trust you.'

Another sigh. 'You're right, but he's so cute.'

'What about marriage counselling?'

'I don't believe in shrinks, you know that.'

'It's not a shrink, really, it's someone to talk to.'

She was becoming more irritated.

'Why don't you and Nice see a counsellor? You two don't seem so happy nowadays.'

She had struck a nerve with her very special brand of Missy-ness.

'We're not talking about me. Go ahead, sleep with Francis. I just hope the sex is worth it.'

With that I got up and left. Her car and driver took me

home. I was upset and anxious and wanted to call Nice. If Missy had noticed our relationship troubles then it was obvious something needed to be done. I needed to know what he was thinking. Maybe I was about to become a single girl again.

CHAPTER SIX

Coupledom

Nice had been avoiding me — headaches, work, whatever he could come up with. But when I got home from Missy's, I found Nice lying on my couch, watching TV with Kitty. Trouble was, we hadn't planned to spend the night together. Sure it was nice that he'd surprised me by letting himself in with the keys I'd given him. Well, to be honest, I'd have preferred it if he'd called first, but I was always so happy to see him that wasn't a big deal.

We smooched on the couch for a bit and then moved to the bedroom. We smooched on the bed and then got under the covers, when something happened. Or rather, it didn't happen. It un-happened. Which had never happened before. We were both quiet for a while, lying in the dark.

'Is something wrong?' I asked, turning on my side and propping myself up on one elbow.

' "Wrong" is really not a good word to use in these moments,' said Nice.

'I take your point. Okay. Um, how are you?' I asked.

'I'm fine. We don't have to talk about it. I'm just tired.' Nice sighed.

'You did seem a little, um, distant when I got home,' I said.

'I was expecting you to be here. Not that you have to tell me what you're doing every night. It just felt a little weird, that's all. To be here and you weren't here. It made me

181

KIM IZZO *and* CERI MARSH

realize that I'd like to be here when you're not here and have it not be weird.'

'Well, the only way I can imagine that is if we were living together,' I started laughing and then realized that Nice wasn't. 'Oh. That's what you meant. You want to live together.'

Now Nice propped himself up on one elbow and smiled. 'Yes, I do. We've been together for more than a year now. We're together all the time, I'm tired of us both dragging all our stuff back and forth across the city. I want to have all our stuff in one place.'

'It's not so much stuff to drag around. Contact lens stuff and the Pill . . .'

Nice rolled onto his back again. He pulled the covers up.

'It's just that after my experience with Groovy . . . It was such a disaster living with him and then splitting up.'

'I'm not Groovy,' said Nice. His voice was getting hard.

'I know you're not. I guess I'm still not ready.'

We lay there in silence. I felt lonely and didn't know what to do for myself let alone how to make Nice feel better somehow. There were suddenly miles between us rather than the couple of inches that separated us in my bed. Eventually we fell asleep.

Coupledom

The Fabulous Girl loves being in love, and often for her love can best be realized in a long-term relationship. She values the closeness that comes with relationships that last and she doesn't stop behaving with decorum as her romance ages. Coupledom creates a variety of challenges that can only be met with experience. Not to say that it gets easier with time and age, but time and age do help the FG take things in her stiletto stride. As well as contending with her own beau, an FG must also interact with her friends' men, and her own list of ex-boyfriends.

Keeping It Up

Just because your relationship has reached a serious commitment plateau doesn't mean that your sex life has to level off. Sex is central to a happy relationship. Anyone who says it isn't, isn't having a lot of good sex. But relationships do change and you may have to remind yourself of what you found sexy about your partner when you were first together. Keeping sex vital in your relationship makes both of you feel sexy and important.

HOT LUNCH

Sex during the day is important in a relationship. It says, 'We're not just doing it because we happen to be in bed together – either at night or first thing in the morning – but we're doing it because we're spontaneously drawn to each other.' Of course, it's inconvenient, but that's part of what makes it good. You might have to cancel a meeting to do it. Call him at work and ask him if he can meet you at home for lunch. Or if he works in an office with good sound-proofing and a door (with a lock), you could pay him a surprise visit at work.

THE SWING SHIFT

A relationship is a living thing and although most patterns emerge within the first few months – sometimes it seems like just weeks – they are not set in stone. The balance of affection can alter over time. It's hard to pinpoint why, but it does. You can be looking at the man you thought you'd chew your own right arm off for and suddenly feel, 'Whatever . . .' You will love him, still love having sex with him, but it just doesn't feel as desperate anymore. Which is good. Now you can calm down and enjoy things more. Unfortunately, most men will perceive this shift – just as you would if you went from being the princess of the relationship to simply the girl-friend. Nobody likes losing status. But the worst thing to do in this situation is to overanalyze it. Try to enjoy the shift and remember that things can always change again. Which is pretty exciting when you think about it.

COMPETITIVE COMPLAINING

A relationship can only last if both halves of a couple are as comfortable playing a supporting role as they are playing the lead. For an FG this can be tricky, as our girl is usually a bit of a star and is often attracted to equally charismatic men; and while this makes for excellent casting when things are going well, it can be a tragedy when things go wrong. When your husband comes home after the day from hell – trapped in bad traffic in the morning, long queues at the bank, computer breakdown at work, tomato sauce down his shirt at lunch – don't scold him for not making the bed this morning.

And really don't take this opportunity to whine about your day. Resist getting into competitive complaining. You'll be surprised at how much better you feel about your own problems by being sympathetic about someone else's. You must go into caretaker mode and offer to mix him a drink while he tells you all about it. And likewise, you should be able to expect that your man will do the same for you.

So SORRY

Women need apologies. Men seem to be able to go about their business after a snarl and can wait for days to revisit the subject of the argument. An FG could more easily flap her arms until she flew to Australia. She must have a resolution to an argument, and she must have it as soon after the argument as possible. Until she has it, she will be unable to do just about anything else. To achieve satisfaction, then, an FG may need to shift her sense of what goes into an apology. Of course, what you really want after a dispute is for your man to realize he was wrong, to appreciate why you were right and to suffer over the pain the argument inflicted upon you. Alas, this is rarely how it goes. In fact, it almost never does. You may never resolve the misunderstanding. It is far more productive to apologize for the fact of the fight than to struggle for perfect mutual understanding. And if you are on the receiving end of an apology which simply says, 'Baby, I'm sorry we fought, I hate to upset you,' you should accept this with grace and move on. Never make a man – or anyone really – regret putting himself out to apologize to you. He won't do it again.

That Long-Distance Feeling

LONG-DISTANCE RELATIONSHIP

We've all heard the refrain that long-distance relationships never work. Yet for many FGs they are inevitable. Why? Because the FG loves to travel and so will often meet desirable men from other cities and countries. What's more, the type of men she gravitates to tend to be worldly and thereby inclined to do some travelling themselves. No matter how she meets Juan, Jorge, Guiseppe or Vladimir, the FG must never abandon the long-distance romance without dabbling a bit first. Distance is simply not a good enough reason to turn down a handsome man, not to mention a free place to stay in a foreign port. Besides, there are times in an FG's life when being 'together' while 'apart' is the most desirable relationship of all. This unconventional couple can have a deeply intense and romantic time together. They will always be thrilled to see each other and will have time set aside just for the occasion. And better yet, when Juan goes home, the FG gets her much-loved space back to herself, which gives her more time to pursue other goals. And she can enjoy the phone sex and the pining a bit.

Of course, while the honeymoon phase for this couple lasts longer, if neither party is willing to move it will eventually end. You may begin to resent him for not being around. You may get sick of going to events alone. Or one of you may meet someone else who does live nearby.

PARTNERS WHO TRAVEL

The FG who loves a man who travels a lot for work may feel that she is living in a long-distance relationship even if they share a home. There are three stages of separation. First, you miss him. It's that yearning, heartachy feeling, those late-night calls from hotel rooms, and back again to that phone sex. Second, you get angry. Enough time has passed that you're bored with phone sex and want the real deal. You're fed up with doing everything at home by yourself. You wonder what the hell is he doing out there without you. Third is relief. Eventually you forget you live with someone and rearrange the furniture or the kitchen cupboards. Then when he's back and he tries to put the cornflakes away, you have to tell him 'We don't put that there anymore.' This is the stage when you don't actually want him back.

Types of careers where this is an issue: touring musicians, authors, actors, salesmen and, of course, high finance – if your boyfriend gets thrown in the slammer for insider trading.

When an FG is the one frequently on the road, she may find these separations a little less painful. It's just not as hard being the one who is jetting off (even if the destination is not always glamorous). She may still miss her mate like crazy but she does have the distraction of change that travel brings with it. Maintaining some kind of schedule of contact is a good way of normalizing what can be a stressful arrange-ment. Make a deal that you'll always chat before bedtime (or whenever). Try to invite him along on trips when it makes sense. Remember to give yourself a bit of time to adjust to being back home after a trip. Particularly if you are away for more than a couple of weeks, you can count on at least one silly fight to pop up in the first few days of your return. It just goes likes that. The tension created by being reunited is romantic but also discombobulating.

A Moveable Beast

You've always wanted to be a talent agent in Los Angeles – problem is, you live in Grimsby. So you've been slogging it out in the local scene. Then lo and behold, one Friday afternoon you get the call from Hollywood. ICM wants you, they really want you. You jump, you shout, you say yes. Then reality hits you – you'll have to move. But will your live-in man, Wilhelm, move too? He's doing well at his job, but is his career in demand in LA? Can he get the necessary immigration papers? Is your relationship over?

This type of major life decision requires true fabulous finessing. While you want to celebrate, buying Wilhelm dinner out at a five-star eatery is not the way to tell him your news. Tell him at home, when you're alone. Chances are you've been communicating your dream to Wilhelm for your entire relationship so the LA move shouldn't come as a shock. He'll probably be thrilled that your dreams are coming true, but then he will naturally think about where it all leaves him.

The FG needs to ask:
- How significant is this relationship?
- Is Wilhelm the man she sees being with for the rest of her life?
- Would she sacrifice her career for him?
- Would a long distance relationship work?
- Can she reasonably ask him to quit his career for hers?

Only when these questions are answered – and it will take more than a few conversations with her beau to do this – will she know what the future of the relationship holds.

HIS MOVE

An FG loves adventure and therefore will love to be involved with a man whose career keeps him on the move. Be careful, however, not to jeopardize your own career to accommodate his. If he's landed a job that will take him to Venice for a year, you may decide that a year away from the intensity of your career will be an oasis. Just remember to take the long view. What if you break up in the middle of his three-year contract in Hong Kong? If the move is within your own country, then you need only consider how such a change will affect your job, your friendships and so on. If the move is bigger – to another country – you need to talk about a bigger commitment. Of course, marriage may be necessary for immigration reasons – to live and work in a foreign country you're going to need to take the proper legal avenues – but marriage also makes it very clear where you both think your relationship is going. Whether you get engaged or simply discuss what kind of commitment you're making to each other, you must know the score before moving. Don't leave home without it.

You Do What?

FG aren't conventional women. They arrange their lives to suit themselves rather than to meet social expectations. Which isn't to say that it's not difficult being a maverick all the time. You and your man are madly in love, you spend time together almost every day, you know that he's the one you're going to get old with. You just don't live together. This may be the perfect set-up for you, the insomniac, and your early-bird boyfriend, but you may catch more than a little flack from the rest of the world. It may be hard for people to recognize your relationship as a committed one if you and your man aren't cohabiting. Don't feel like you need to give an explanation to the world about how you organize your personal life. Employ the turnaround technique: 'It's great, we have the best of both worlds. How is your relationship?' You don't need to defend your relationship, just enjoy it.

Weathering a Crisis in Your Partner's Life

We all dream of finding unconditional love. As we grow up, we think that we won't settle down until we find a person who can accept all our faults and shortcomings. But what's an FG to do if she finds she's not up to that task herself? You're with the guy who for years has seemed like Mr Right. The two of you are compatible in every way. And then disaster strikes – him, not you. While your career is on the rise, his begins to plummet. Your financial future looks rock solid and his is disintegrating. You noticed that he's started to look a little shabby when he heads out the door in the morning. Over dinner, when you ask him what he's got going on at work, he mumbles and changes the subject. He's withdrawn and doesn't seem interested in going out anymore.

Loyalty is a prized quality in an FG and she won't want to point out to her man that things are looking bleak. But some situations call for a cold, hard look rather than rose-tinted glasses. Sit down and have a frank but supportive conversation with your mate. He may be grateful to you for acknowledging what is obvious to you both: that he's in a bad situation. Ask him what he'd like to do about his predicament and whether or not there's anything you can do to help. Offer suggestions: let him know you're happy to stop going out for dinner for a few months to save money, tell him it's more romantic to you to stay at home anyway.

You may find, however, that your man just doesn't want to

confront his problems, and he doesn't want you looking at them either. He doesn't have to share everything with you, but if he won't talk about how he lost his job and he's been out of work for more than a couple of months, it's time to re-evaluate. His life doesn't have to match yours, but you do have to know what's going on.

WHEN TO GET INVOLVED

Months have ticked by and still your man hasn't found a job. You know this is not his normal modus operandi, he's simply in a rut. But the rut has grown tiresome. You're bored of his whining, his inability to get off the couch let alone get a job interview. And worse, you learn that he has a potential job but hasn't bothered to follow it up. What happens next is up to you. Can you call his pal at that top-level legal firm and invite him for dinner, thereby putting your man in the path of opportunity? Of course you can, but know that your boyfriend will recognize why you've made the invitation and he may be riled. You're going too far if you tell the pal that your boyfriend is down on his luck and needs a break. That is humiliation and not a fabulous thing to do.

SURPRISE ENDING

If after much soul searching your man decides what he really needs is a big change in career, you will of course be delighted that he's finally found inspiration. Of course, the shift he's imagining may affect both of you. If he's decided he can't stomach another day at his law firm and what he's always secretly wanted to do is to raise llamas, then it's going to be a change in lifestyle for both of you. It's not his bank account you fell in love with, but if one half of a relationship makes a radical life change, then it's to be expected that the romance may be seriously tested. You may feel that you can support this shift in focus but only as a friend. You don't want to move to the country and must sadly end the relationship. Who knows, maybe you *can* also get your head around those early morning trips out to the barn.

Break Up & Make Up

THE FABULOUS GIRL PARADE

He dumped you and broke your heart. Then just as you feel like you're getting back on your feet, the call comes. He can't believe the mistake he's made, he's sorry and he wants to get back together. It is reasonable that an FG who has been dumped and then 'won back' by the ex will have difficulties with trust during the early days of round two. The Fabulous Girl will need to vent her anger and have several rounds of reconciliation chatter prior to accepting the invitation to get back together. But then, once she's back with her boyfriend, she needs a parade. Yes, this may need to be explained to him, preferably during the discussion phase, but it is expected. The FG's ex-now-boyfriend needs to be mindful of his FG's pride. She may be worried that she's foolish to trust him or that he will leave her again. (Which often happens in these scenarios.)

So. He'll need to throw a parade. This can take many forms. The obvious daily parades of I love you and You're wonderful are a must. Small gifts are also good. We're not talking about flashy displays of money, but of thoughtfulness and effort. Flowers, cards, romantic dinners and so on are the kind of thing that will be useful.

The back together backlash

If you are going back, you need to think about whether or not you can let go of the anger you felt over being dumped. Can you really be in the new relationship if you'll just keep taking it out on your ex-now-boyfriend. Try to get all the serious talking done in the early days of negotiating. Why are things different now, what really happened during your breakup and so on. Then put your concerns on the shelf and just see how it goes. Round two can't work if you don't give it a chance to be fun and romantic. But be honest about your feelings. If things are unresolved, talk it over as calmly as possible rather than letting things bubble up. 'Did you leave a centimetre of milk in the carton? That's just like when you broke up with me' – isn't appropriate.

If the FG is the one asking her ex to come back, then she must expect a certain amount of flack from him too. She's obliged to take angry sessions and negotiations, and she also needs to put on a parade for him.

There must be 50 ways

When you've got to go, you've got to go. Probably you should have left three months ago, but you thought it might work out. It didn't. You let your boyfriend know that you were tired of waiting for marriage and kids and he didn't bite. You realized that the crush on the guy at work was getting out of control. Whatever the circumstances are, you need to make a move. No matter how bad things are (unless you walked in on him and another woman) you must have a breakup conversation. You may like the dramatic flair that a note on the kitchen table has, but it's just not fabulous. Breakups are hard, but you must be brave and do it in person. Even if the very next thing you do is call a cab to stay at a friend's place.

THE FAKE BREAKUP

It may look like a breakup, sound like a breakup and even smell like a breakup, but it's not – it's a fake break. If you speak with your ex more than once a week, see each other at least once a week and sleep with each other once a month, then you are involved in a fake break. This is, of course, painful if you are the one who was dumped, but if you were the one who did the dumping it is downright mean. You may think you are weaning your ex off you, and naturally if he is broken-hearted he will encourage this line of reasoning. But as the person who wanted the separation, you must be the stronger party. You may subconsciously be hoping that the two of you can remain friends, that you can keep the things you love about him in your life. But if he's still in love with you, it's just not fair. It's selfish.

GET OUT

Live-in couples are obviously committed. This situation only makes breaking up more complicated. If the Fabulous Girl moved into her boyfriend's place, then the place remains his after they split. Remember, it is always better to find a new place as a couple rather than move into someone else's abode.

So there you are, the FG in the midst of a huge fight with the boyfriend. It's ugly, he's wrong, you're right, he's not listening, he loses his temper and out flies from his twisted mouth, 'Get out.' Mortified, the FG gathers a few things, and calling her best friend, spends the night elsewhere. It would be wrong to stay and fight it out. If tempers have flared this high, then reason is obviously out the window – clearer heads will prevail in the cold dawn. Right?

Wrong. The FG did the right thing by leaving – after all, she did what he asked. But when she goes back to their shared place the following day, what does she do if she opens the door only to find every single thing she owns is packed and waiting at the door? Turns out he didn't actually want you to leave, he just wanted a reaction, but when you left he felt abandoned.

The boyfriend was so angry that he stayed up all night packing the FG's life away. Now she has two options. One, if the relationship is over then she can take solace in knowing that she has a lot less work to do. Packing is such a bore, isn't it? Two, if the relationship can be mended and he's apologized or perhaps you both have, then let him unpack your things.

Cheating Bastard

Despite the Fabulous Girl's many charms, she may still one day end up with a cheating bastard boyfriend or husband. Unfortunately, it is true that the FG's beauty and grace are not protection against such a man. What does the FG do if she comes home early from work or that weekend with the girls only to discover Bingo in bed with another woman?

The FG, as difficult as it may be, does not lose it. She doesn't scream or throw anything. She is the perfect picture of calm and good deportment. Remember girls, they're scum, so let them writhe. The FG will instead grab a chair or lean against the wall, arms crossed, and stare. Wait for *him* to utter the first words. And don't think you should leave the room so *she* can get dressed with dignity. No way. No matter how much it kills you, it's killing them more. In fact, your stoic silence is gut-wrenchingly loud to the cheaters. What will happen is he will blurt out explanations or apologies and she will try to hide. If he asks you to leave, refuse. A simple, calm 'No, I don't think I will' should suffice. If she gets hysterical, let her. In fact, don't bother to look her in the face at all. It's as though she's not there – after all this is between you and him. Once she's gone, then walk out of the room, sit in the living room and wait for him to come to you to talk. The rest will unfold as you see fit. But this way the FG will maintain control of the situation.

How you handle this domestic issue in public is as vital as how you cope in private. A certain movie-star Fabulous Girl is a stellar example of grace under pressure. Her equally famous boyfriend was arrested one night on Sunset Boulevard, having engaged in sexual acts with a hooker. His mug shot found its way onto every newsstand and current affairs show. Yet our FG remained silent, choosing to keep the incident between her and the boyfriend. She issued a simple public statement, but that was that. And showed up on his arm at a film premiere later.

IT GETS WORSE

Even in the worst-case scenario – when you know the woman in question – staying in control still works like a charm. You'll just need to have two conversations instead of one. Each one separately, please. The female betrayal being worse somehow, this conversation requires its own time and place.

What if after all the dust settles you opt to forgive if not forget your friend? Often an FG can do without a certain kind of man, but a best friend is more difficult to replace. Of course, we're assuming the friend is repentant and misses the FG too. If the two women decide to remain friends, they will have to endure the whispers of others. This will be particularly hard on the FG since she is the wounded party, and she will find that strangers will have an opinion on her situation. Even other friends will not fathom how you could still be friends with *her*. The FG must ignore these people.

She simply refuses to discuss it. If the FG is willing to socialize and be friends with this woman, then the rest of FG's social circle must also accept her. It is the gracious thing to do.

Ex Marks the Spot

It doesn't matter if the Fabulous Girl has one ex or a list of exes that, if read, would have the music start to signal her exit stage left. These men can sometimes still figure prominently in her life. Feelings for them, be it anger or love, may even lie dormant and bubble to the surface in unexpected moments. An FG must learn when it's time to bow out gracefully from maintaining a friendship with an ex, and when being mates is just dandy, thank you.

EX-RATED

There are many occasions in life when we get caught off guard, but few will be as fraught as those accidental encounters with an ex. What makes these meetings worse is seeing him with his new gal. But be careful, how you react will say much about the state of your feelings.

1. If it's over, it's over. So why are you frequenting Bingo's fave bar? When you keep 'running into' him, it will be obvious that you have unfinished business. If that is so, then ask to see him alone and speak your piece. Then move on. After that, attempting to make your meetings seem co-incidental is simply stalking. And if both of you refuse to give up your pasta joint, be prepared to have each other and the new dates in your lives.

2. He's unavoidable. You were both invited to the wedding/cocktail party/birthday celebration long before you

197

split up. It's not obvious which of you has more claim on the event and so you're both going to go. You must do your best to be civilized. But you must also do your best to look as good as you ever have. It's time to employ the Fuck-Him Dress, with a salon blowout for good measure. Have a plan for the night. Don't drink too much – three champagne cocktails and you may suddenly feel like it's the perfect time to rehash your breakup. And have an exit plan in case you decide you can't handle it. Discuss a subtle hand signal with a close friend. A tug on your ear and you're both heading for the door.

3. What if you are the dreaded ex? You know you broke his heart and he is pining, so guilt may induce you to avoid him at all costs. Not a bad decision – unless he spots you doing the avoiding and then you are the boor. Once you've made eye contact, you must acknowledge him no matter how awkward it is. You should muster the courage to say hello and then move on as quickly as possible.

4. Can't stand the sight of Felix? The only good thing you got out of that relationship is that you got out? Then feel free to snub. Avoid meeting his eye and pretend not to see him. If he does approach, say hello and continue on your way. You are not obliged to engage in conversation, nor do you have to invite him to sit down with you.

WHEN YOUR EX BECOMES THE STAR

When your relationship with Bingo ended, you thought you might never see him again. After all, there were times when it seemed as if he was never going to come down from his attic science lab. Then one day you're flipping around the TV and there he is, accepting the Nobel Prize for his work on particle theory. All the attention paid to your former lover can have personal ramifications – especially if you dumped him because he never seemed to get himself together. If he is a particularly wounded soul, he may even relish his new achievements and seek to rub them in your powdered nose. How you learn of his successes tells a lot of how he still feels about you and your breakup.

1. You read about Bingo in the press. He's over it and is now enjoying the bikini-clad crowd in Cannes. Now is a good time to get over him.

2. You 'accidentally' bump into one of *his* friends, who fills you in. This may not be idle gossip – your ex may or may not have encouraged his mate to spill the beans. Or his loyal friend just wants you to know what a mistake you made in dumping Bingo. Either way, it's a power play and he just wants you to be aware.

3. Your mutual friends tell you all about it so that you don't have to read about it later. They may be trying to protect you. Time to reiterate that you dumped him and you're happy about the money, fame and social life he now has. Chances are he'll be getting a blow-by-blow account of your reaction to his success from the friends, so how you come across in Scenario 2 or 3 is vital for ensuring that Bingo believes there are no sour grapes.

4. Bingo calls you every time something great happens. He signs a recording contract. He's got a new producer who worked on the Stones' last album. He's touring with Bowie. Bingo wants you to feel really, really bad about dumping him. He wants you to have regrets. And yes, part of him is still in love with you.

Other People's Breakups

A breakup in your social circle is a stress for everyone, not just the couple that is splitting. Naturally, when people who seemed well suited can't keep it together, it makes you wonder what it takes to keep it together. Do you and your man have what it takes? And how is he feeling, exactly, about your relationship? As best as you can, try not to make this the moment you choose to have a big relationship talk. It will, of course, be the most tempting thing in the world. And you won't be able to avoid talking about the broken relationship. But try not to draw parallels.

Breakups never affect only the two people directly involved – there's a whole network of relationships rocked by the disintegration of one. And the longer a couple has been together, the more their separation will send ripples through their social circle. Of course, well-mannered couples try to end their relationships with as much grace as they can muster. But some etiquette pressure does fall on their peers, and there are rules of decorum to help ease the stress.

If you only ever really liked Fred and never could stand Ginger, then you don't have a problem. You can just enjoy Fred's company and allow your connection with Ginger to fade away. But if you've always palled around with both of them, you have a few duties. First, you must immediately let both parties know you will continue to be their pal. The newly broken-up will have some anxiety over whose friends are whose. Make it easier and let them know you're not taking sides.

And while you aren't obliged to keep the splitters away from each other, in the early days it's diplomatic to warn each of them if they're invited to the same event. Obviously, we're talking about large gatherings not tiny dinner parties, where only a fool would invite both residents of Splitsville.

Which brings up the next issue: never interfere in someone else's breakup. Don't try to fix it because you really miss spending time with Bob and Bonnie. If they want to get back together, they will; your faking an invite to a party only to shove the two of them together in a closed room is the stuff of sitcoms not fabulousness. And don't fall into the trap of acting as a mediator on behalf of Bob or vice versa. Bob and Bonnie can talk to each other themselves.

If you are in the rare position of being equally close with each part of a relationship on the rocks, your diplomacy will be tested. You've known and adored both Bingo and Fifi for years and now they're in a trial separation. Fifi's been seeing someone and Bingo is broken-hearted. Of course, Fifi will be dying to talk about her new romance, and as a friend you will feel compelled to indulge her. While you needn't make the new man's name *verboten*, it's not a good idea to be a cheer-leader for this affair either. If Fifi is on the rebound – and she likely is – she doesn't need any help getting carried away. And since Fifi and Bingo may still reunite, you may as well not invest too much emotional energy into the other man.

Finally, refrain from discussing the comings and goings of one half of the breakup to the other. You can listen (prefer-ably neutrally) to Ginger analyze all of Fred's shortcomings. But you may not, ever, add, 'Well, he certainly looks cosy in his new romance, so I guess New Girl doesn't mind that he doesn't pick up his dirty socks.'

Other Women

NEW FG IN TOWN

There are certain people who simply have no manners when it comes to meeting those who are new to their social set. It goes like this: Guy in an established clique brings a new date to a function. As the group reconfigures to make space for the new person, some people seem unable to make the transition with grace. Unfortunately, this lack of hospitality can come in the form of aggressive flirting: bitches behaving badly. A few rules need to be adhered to:

1. Back off. Whether the man was the love of your life or just a two-month fling, if he's at a gathering with his new girl, you have no business rubbing your shoulders up and down his (and knocking his girlfriend off her Jimmy Choos). And even if the man has only ever been a friend, you still must alter your behaviour around his date or you risk appearing (a) insensitive or (b) moronic. No dramatic displays such as blowing kisses, winking or hugs that end up dipping your old friend to the ground.

2. Zip your lip. One of the worst catty callings in life is gossip. Yes, we all love to do it and hear it, but it should always be done well away from its subject matter. A group of women huddled at a party discussing the new girl within earshot, and in an unflattering manner, is thoroughly tacky. Why not include her in your conversational circle instead of analyzing her outfit?

3. Don't judge. If your good pal Betsy has an older man on her arm don't assume (a) he's her sugar daddy or (b) she needs a father figure. Perhaps this older man and younger woman are in love. Be happy for your friend. If you swallow your surprise and engage him in conversation, maybe you'll discover the nature of their relationship.

4. Don't stoop. If you are a victim of such cattiness, there is little that can be done but ignore it. Don't stoop to making nasty retaliatory remarks. Of course, you can sweetly whisper about it into your date's ear and laugh out loud.

THE EX

As a wise FG once noted, there is always one ex who broke his heart who he just won't quite get over. That annoying one who got away, and if she hadn't, he'd still be with her instead of you. Suppose your beau is really close, even best friends, with his ex. That's right. She's the one he calls when he's fought with you, she's going to be advising him on how to deal with your insecurity over *her* or whatever else. What's an FG to do? Bite it. There's little you can do other than befriend her yourself. If you and she becomes close then she's likely to be less of an issue. But if you really can't get over their closeness (and many upstanding FGs can't) or she won't let you two alone, then you may want to change boyfriends. Of course, if she's in another city, that helps!

I was halfway through an item on a new night club when the call from Missy came. It was in those moments that I would curse the magazine for being too cheap to have call-display phones on every desk. You'd pick up the phone thinking it was going to be a publicist you could blow off in less than three minutes, and instead it was your best friend who needed to have a serious talk that would be better suited to a bar. And Missy is not easily gotten off the phone once she's on. Never mind my deadline – when she's got a crisis, everything else must be dropped.

'I think Joe is going to leave me.'

'Missy? Is that you? Let me just save this work. Okay. Hello. Now, what are you talking about? What have you done?'

'Why do you assume it's my fault?'

'Um, because you were about to get it on with Francis last week, maybe?'

At that moment, I swivelled in my chair to see that Cheryl was standing at the edge of my cubicle, smiling and nodding as if she, too, were amazed at Missy's recent behaviour. I smiled weakly at her even though it really drives me crazy when people do that. I mean, she could see that I was on the phone. Clearly, she was listening in on the conversation.

'Just a second, Missy.' I covered the receiver with my hand. 'Hi, Cheryl.'

'Just wondering when the entertainment listings are going to be finished? Everything else in that section is ready to go.'

'I'm sorry, I thought it was going to be ready tomorrow—'

'But then you got busy doing another piece for the paper?' Cheryl raised an eyebrow.

'Within an hour, I swear. You know I'm never late with my copy.'

Cheryl just nodded lazily and didn't move. 'I know. Look, I'm not trying to give you a hard time. Just because he doesn't mention it, don't think Bradley hasn't noticed how much work you're doing for the paper. Don't give him any reason to think you're slacking here.'

I nodded and held up the phone. 'You're right. Thanks. I've had this person on hold for quite a while now, Cheryl, I'd better get back to it. Don't worry about the listings. End of the day for sure.'

Finally, she left. I was worried about what she'd said about my work and Bradley noticing that my mind was elsewhere lately, but I had to put it aside to deal with Missy at that moment.

'Sorry, got to go. Maybe we should just meet later to talk about all this?'

'Okay. Where shall we meet? The usual? Joe is playing football tonight, so we could meet for dinner?'

'Great. Do you want to call Eleanor and see if she's free, too? I'll see you at around 7:30?'

I got to Dominick's a little late because I was finishing up that listing for Cheryl. The girls were already there. Once we'd ordered, we got down to business.

'Now, why do you think that Joe is going to leave you?' I asked.

'Because he can tell she's not in love with him anymore?' proposed Eleanor. With pregnancy, she had become even more frank. Which for Eleanor was saying something.

'I do love him! I know I've been a bit crazy lately. But I love him, and I do want my marriage to work. I've been so focused on his faults and the whole Francis issue that I hadn't noticed that Joe hasn't exactly been happy with *me* either. I've decided I don't want to lose him!' Missy's eyes were filling up with tears.

Eleanor and I both reached across the table to hold Missy's hands. Of course, I was filled with sympathy for Missy's anguish, but I also got a lump in my throat thinking that maybe I was going to lose Nice by expecting things between us to be perfect before we moved in together.

'I'm sorry,' said Eleanor. 'I was being stupid. It's my pregnancy mouth. I know you love Joe.'

'Maybe you just need to create a little romance with Joe,' I said.

'What do you mean?' asked Missy.

'Well, I mean don't wait for him to make a move. You can do a little seducing of your own.'

'Exactly,' said Eleanor. 'Turn up the heat a little, Missy.'

'I don't know how. Joe has always been the one to do that stuff, you know? He pursued me.' Missy looked miserable.

So we came up with a plan to rekindle the romance in Missy's marriage. By the end of the meal, we felt as if we'd solved the whole thing. I was glad that she seemed to be on the right track in her relationship. It seemed obvious to me that Missy's crush on Francis was simply her way of avoiding going deeper with Joe. She didn't really want to have an affair at all, she was just afraid of the real intimacy that she could have with her husband. And I was feeling a little better about Nice as well. Surely the awkward feeling between us was something that I could overcome with a little romance? Or could it? Maybe I was only good at giving out advice and not at taking it. Missy's driver took us home in the new Mercedes, and she came along for the ride. As Eleanor got out of the car, she leaned over for goodnight kisses.

'Whatever you do, Miss, don't lose this car, I mean marriage . . .'

Missy called me the next day to tell me that our plan was working well already. When Joe had got home that night, he'd found that Missy had poured him a hot bath and had a drink waiting, too. After sitting on the edge of the tub for a bit listening to how Joe had scored the winning goal, Missy had pulled off her dress, stepped into the bath with him and told him she thought he just might score again that night.

CHAPTER SEVEN

Weddings and Divorce

I don't know why people think that weddings are romantic. Of course, I get how they're romantic for the couple getting married, but even they usually seem more stressed than smitten.

I wasn't looking forward to Helen's wedding, to be honest. I knew it would be beautiful. Helen and her fiancé, Sam, have excellent taste and the money to pull off a great-looking wedding. Which in my experience is no small thing. How many weddings have I been to where you can tell they spent a lot and it's still tacky as hell? Too many.

Nice and I were a little on edge. The conversation about moving in together still hung uncomfortably over us. I was trying hard to show Nice that just because I wasn't ready to shack up didn't mean that I wasn't in love with him. We walked through the entrance of the museum where Helen and Sam's wedding was about to take place, and I had to admit it was beautiful. The room was lit with a million candles and there were sprays of white flowers on every surface. As we found our seats I said, 'Remember the last wedding we were at?'

Nice just frowned, suggesting that he didn't remember.

'Missy's wedding? Where we met?'

'Oh, yeah.'

Okay, so much for that.

The ceremony was the kind I like, short and traditional.

211

There's nothing worse than those couples who insist on writing their own vows and end up promising to make each other banana milkshakes and the like. Helen looked beautiful, and the way Sam looked at her during the ceremony was amazing. Did Nice and I look at each other like that? Did we feel the things you're supposed to feel? I just didn't know, and I didn't want to look over at him.

Helen and Sam were smart enough to hire a great band, and as soon as dinner was finished people were up on the dance floor. Things started to thaw a little between Nice and me while we glided across the room.

'This is how I started to fall for you, when we first danced,' I said. And he did seem to remember that. We danced over to Missy and Joe only to find them bickering.

'Well, I'm pretty sure I noticed you flirting with the waiter,' Joe spat as we danced away.

Just then Eleanor, now eight months pregnant, twirled by us with a grey-bearded gentleman at least a half foot shorter than her. She was gritting her teeth but still smiling as he whirled her around. As she turned I noticed one of the man's hands riding awfully low on her full hips.

The State of Matrimony and Acrimony

The very notion of marriage is an extreme one. A lifetime commitment to another person is one of the biggest moves an FG (or anyone else) can make. What may surprise her most is the size of the gap between her assumptions about what getting married would be like and what reality delivers. The greatest myth that an FG may hold on to is that the wedding is an event that she and her man will share. Hopefully, it is that too, but mostly it is built around clannish impulses and therefore must accommodate many more people than just the couple getting married. And if history teaches us anything it is that the more people involved in any single enterprise, the more the possibility for drama. Lo, the drama of the wedding – the first or the third.

Of course, in the case of multiple marriages, there had to be at least one divorce. Divorces also rarely live up to expectation and, like weddings, involve more people than simply the couple splitting up.

The Proposal: Giving Ultimatums

An FG has to think hard about what she really wants from her life. Because she is so full of energy, she can sometimes trick herself into thinking that she'll get to everything she wants to do eventually. This is almost true. And if it's not, then it's still a great approach to life. But to get the most out of life, one does need goals. As an FG, you see this clearly in your professional life. It's a good idea to apply this same philosophy to your personal life. If you don't seem to care one way or the other about commitment, the man in your life will likely not be compelled to make one. It's important to be honest with yourself and with him about what you really want.

Of course, being in a relationship means making room for someone else's perspective as well. If you always thought you'd be married by the time you were twenty-five but you're almost there and the fantastic guy you're with hasn't asked yet, your life is not a failure. At the same time, FGs shouldn't fall into the trap of being afraid to bring up the subject of marriage for fear of seeming old-fashioned. If you know it's something you need in order to be fulfilled, then you should be clear. For instance, as your relationship is solidifying, you should let him know in objective terms what your perfect situation would be: 'I've always thought it would be ideal to be married sometime in my early thirties.' And ask him how he sees his life unfolding. If he's still not making a move and you're into the second year of your relationship, you should bring it up. As neutrally as you can, ask him how he's feeling about the idea of marriage and how he imagines your relationship developing. And you've got to really listen to the answer. Marriage is hard, and you don't want to convince someone to do it against his will. If he's not making moving-in-together-you're-the-one noises during this conversation, then you'll have to make a stronger statement yourself: 'I love you and want to be with you. I'd like to move on to the next level of commitment. Let's talk about it again in six months and see if we're moving in the same direction.' Present this bit of information calmly. And try to keep the conversation brief.

Do not resort to the age-old tactic of the ultimatum, 'Marry me or else we're through.' No FG would want to enter into a marriage based on a threat. Likewise, be prepared for him to disappoint you. This is one of the toughest love moves to make because through your very desire for more commitment, you may be ending the relationship.

The Prenup

You have some money and some property, be it a home, jewellery, car, whatever. You either earned it yourself or inherited it from your family. Or perhaps you know you are going to inherit in the future. If you are an independent-minded FG, you have gone along for some time considering your assets to be your own. When you become engaged, it's time to reassess both your and your fiancé's feelings about cash. This means discussing the possible end to the relationship. While unpleasant and unromantic, bringing up the topic of a prenuptial agreement is a wise approach to modern marriage. Let's face it: more than 50 per cent of first marriages end in divorce (monetary strife is a leading cause) so you will be saving yourself much grief and anxiety if you deal with your assets prior to marriage.

Asking your mate to sign a prenuptial agreement does not mean you intend to be unfair to him if and when your relationship breaks up. It does mean that the financial terms of a breakup are made clear in advance. Perhaps you'd like to insist that you would only split assets that are accrued during the course of your relationship and that money you had before would automatically go to your children rather than to him? Likewise, you can decide how to divide stocks, retirement plans and other assets in the event of your (or his) death. If you are involved in a family business, without a prenup you may be forced (and therefore force your family) to liquidate the business or enter into a costly buyout of shares with your ex-husband.

There is no sense in mincing words. Take your fiancé out for dinner and inform him you want a prenuptial agreement. How he handles the situation may tell you a lot more about him than you knew before he popped the question. If he refuses, then you may have to reconsider the marriage.

What if he asks you to sign a prenup? Again, it will feel like a hard-hearted move. It presumes a possible end to the relationship when you should be thinking of its success. Nevertheless, he's asking. You have to ask yourself what is really fair. How do you intend to live while you are married? Are you going to give up or take a break from your career? Doing so will put a serious dent in your future earning potential. If you divorce from your wealthy spouse, is it going to seem fair that you then have to go out into the workforce as if it were an even playing field? Think of how your kids may feel shuttling from the home of a wealthy parent back to a poorer parent's place on a Sunday night. Once legal documents have been discussed, it is not the time to get romantic and say that you don't care about his money. He's telling you *he* cares about his money – you may as well, too.

LEGAL EAGLE

If you do decide to go the prenup route, you must negotiate the contract with legal council. Better to spend on this than run up escalating duelling divorce lawyers later. Be firm with your lawyer and encourage your partner to do the same. Lawyers should work toward a document that reflects your wishes as a couple. Lawyers are combative by training and have been known to create bad feelings in couples during the negotiation process. Don't be pushed around. Decide what you and your future husband want and stick to it.

OTHER PRE-WEDDING NEGOTIATIONS

How money will be handled in your marriage is not the only conversation an FG insists on before she walks down the aisle. Don't assume that just because he wants to be your husband he wants to be the father of your children. Likewise, don't assume that he should know by your freewheeling ways that you have no intention of popping out a couple of kids. You should discuss what you both feel about children (if you want them, how many, when you're going to have them) as your relationship is solidifying. Don't wait until the honeymoon.

The Invitation List

The longer an FG puts off getting married, the more complicated her invitation list is going to be. Do you invite his ex-wife and her new husband? Probably not. Do you invite your ex-boyfriend from high school who has since become close with your fiancé? Maybe. You and your betrothed should sit down and have a frank discussion about whom you feel comfortable including in your celebration. You need to be generous with each other. And we don't mean you have to let your husband-to-be invite his ex-girlfriend. We mean that if he feels squeamish about someone on your list, you need to heed his feelings and strike out the offender. That way your mixed feelings can be honoured as well.

WORKMATES

Without a doubt, the Fabulous Girl gets along with nearly everyone in her workplace. However, she does not have to invite them all to her wedding. Collect the home addresses of those you wish to invite and leave it at that. While no one has a right to ask you why they weren't invited (how poor mannered if they do!), if asked, a simple 'It's a very small wedding' should suffice.

If you are the lucky workmate to be invited to the wedding, do not broadcast it around the office or tell the bride-to-be how excited you are about the invitation in the presence of other colleagues in case the others were not invited. This may prove uncomfortable for the bride-to-be.

CHILDREN

If you choose not to have little ones at your wedding, then ensure that when you send out invites you specify, 'Mr and Mrs Thomas,' and not, 'Mr and Mrs Thomas and family.' Please take note that if you receive an invite that does *not* say 'and family,' then your kids are not invited. This can prove tough to communicate, as it seems more and more modern parents find even one day's separation from their little bundles of joy excruciating and may think you improper. However, a formal wedding is no place for toddlers and definitely no place for babies.

If your wishes are ignored and you do have wailing babies in the church, you must not let it get to you. Now is not the time to ask your cousin Rachel to find a babysitter.

OUT-OF-TOWN WEDDINGS

Your oldest friend in the world is getting married in Guam. It's what she's always wanted. You can remember her dreamily describing her future Guam wedding when you were small kids. You were so thrilled for her when she announced her engagement to her long-time boyfriend. And then out of the blue comes the wedding invitation. Sure enough, she has decided to have her big day in Guam – in one month. Eek. Your work schedule is punishing. Your bank account is at a low. What to do? Are you obliged to move heaven and earth to be with your old friend?

Yes and no. Deciding that your wedding is going to be

held far from home automatically means that many of your desired guests won't be able to make it. You're asking them to spend considerable money and effort to make the trip. And the best way to make that a possibility is to give them lots of notice. Even if you're not ready to send out the physical invitations, you should let people know what your plans are as soon as you can. If that's not possible you have to live with the results. Let your friends and family know that although you'd love to have them with you, you will understand if they can't make it. And really mean it.

This means that if close friends RSVP no, because of finances or timing or whatever, you cannot ignore them and remain angry and sulky over it. After all, you decided to do it overseas.

BACKING OUT OF THE INVITATION

You have RSVP'd yes to your friend's long-distance wedding. But as the time grows near, some financial or business fiasco occurs and you realize you're going to have to cancel. This call should be made no later than one month before the wedding so the couple still has time to make adjustments – unless, of course, it is a dire emergency that cannot be helped. Either way, you must inform the couple as soon as you know you will not be able to attend. Just not showing up is inexcusable and there is very little you can do to make it up to your friends.

Elopements

You and the love of your life have decided to take a two-week get-away to Bermuda. It's hot, the sea is frothy and he's never looked better to you. The sex is great, and finally the two of you decide that a life together will be exactly like this every day. So you track down some sort of official, get the local legalities out of the way and there you stand, barefoot on a beach. Ten minutes later you're married! Congrats. You've just saved yourself (and friends and family) a ton of angst and money. However, recognize that some people will be disappointed about not being there. Particularly your mother. How upset you think people will be should determine if you call them immediately afterwards to let them in on your secret or if you wait until you're home and can do it in person.

Either way, you cannot expect the same fuss or deluge of gifts as a traditional wedding would bring. If people do choose to bring or send you a gift, you must follow traditional protocol and send a thank-you note.

If you do think people feel cheated, or if you just want to celebrate, throw a party. People will then feel part of the process even without having borne witness to your vows.

Should You Inform Your Exes?

They can't all live in Texas or any other far flung location. Once you've made all the happy I'm-getting-married calls – to your mother, to your best friend, to the nice people at Vera Wang – you must make a few hard calls. You must contact (or be sure that someone in a good position to do it is going to do it) your most serious ex boyfriends or ex husbands (by serious we mean those you are on friendly terms with). It's not right to let an ex hear about your upcoming marriage through the grapevine. If you want to maintain some kind of relationship with this person, you should deal with it in a straightforward manner. Of course it's not easy, but you need to protect his pride. If you honestly think it would be better coming from someone else then arrange it that way.

YOUR EX'S FAMILY

If you aren't married in your early twenties then you've probably had at least one – and let's face it, probably a lot more than that – other significant relationship before getting engaged. Which in most cases means that you were close not only to that person but also to his friends and maybe even to his family. They may have become as important to you as he was. It's one of the most difficult parts of ending long-term relationships: the corollary breakups with the people in his life. People who never even made you cry. You may try to maintain some of these relationships after your split. Should they, however, be invited to your wedding? This is a tough decision to be made by you and your fiancé. Maybe it's been a long enough period that you have new associations with your ex's mother and you can all be comfortable with her at your wedding. Maybe it's going to quietly annoy your man all day and not be worth the hassle. But what other people think should not come into it: what it looks like to the other guests means nothing next to your own comfort and the comfort of your fiancé.

Fractured Families and Your Wedding

For many a Fabulous Girl the nuclear family was just not a part of her upbringing. On her wedding day she may have to delicately balance the various factions of what is her very modern-day family – parents who are divorced, remarried and the like.

221

MUM AND DAD

(The FG may want to photocopy this for her parents.) So he left her for another woman? Sure it hurt, probably still stings a bit, but wasn't it also five or ten years ago? Parents need to be aware that the wedding day of their child is just that, and not another opportunity to put their kid in the middle. Even if Mum can't stand the sight of her ex-spouse, she's hurting her daughter by refusing to attend the ceremony or reception. Mum must go to both. Mum must smile and be pleasant. And Mum absolutely must say hello to her ex. She must stand in the receiving line. She does not, however, have to pose in the same photo unless her child has worked that out in advance.

STEPPARENTS

Of course, you must include both your parents' new partners. And yes, you must ask the stepparents to be in the wedding photos. Some divorced people are in so much denial about their ex's current status that it is wise to remind them.

THE GIVEAWAY

Haven't seen your dad since you were six? You don't have to forgo being walked down the aisle just because you can't go the traditional father-daughter route. Feel free to be creative with who walks you down the aisle. Your mum? A favourite uncle? Even a best friend (who doesn't have to be male). Since the assumption is that the father walks his daughter down the aisle, even if you're not close but Dad is still invited, you do need to let him know that you feel more comfortable with an alternative arrangement. Of course, if he has been a completely absent parent then you do not have to inform him of any plans.

TOASTING

If this ritual is tense with both parents and stepparents in attendance, a slight manoeuvring of the speech order can satisfy all parties. The father of the bride is traditionally the first to toast the new couple, and there is no reason to alter this. If you are also close to your stepfather, by all means include him in the toasting lineup. But in order to make a distinction for your biological father (if you wish to), have your stepdad speak one person away from your dad – your father, the chief bridesmaid, then your stepfather. This is all dependent on family dynamics. Again, warn everyone in advance of how you intend to organize your toasts so that there are no surprises. And by all means, allow Mum to say a few words too, especially if you are father-free.

I DO, AGAIN

Second marriages can be fraught with tension if stepchildren are involved. Witness a certain knighted 1960s pop idol whose daughter refused to attend his second wedding. If you are entering marriage for the second time, you must invite your children even if you know they'll refuse – just think of the extra cash you're saving at meal-time. Always make sure that the kids of a combining family are given equal billing in terms of their seating, both at the ceremony and at the reception. You can't put your kids at the head table and banish your new hubby's kids to Outer Siberia. There is also a balancing act in terms of attendants, and it is wise to invite kids from both sides to step into the bridesmaid/usher role, even if they decline.

FG AS NEW STEPKID

Even if you hate your future stepparent, you should behave like a grown-up and be at the wedding to support your parent in his or her new marriage. You don't have to have Sunday lunch every week, but you can show up this one day. You may grow to become close to your step, and then you will be glad you didn't behave foolishly on the wedding day.

ABSENT PARENTS

If the FG has no contact with either parent or if contact is particularly strained, she is not obliged to invite that parent to her wedding. A very famous television star who married an even more famous movie star was criticized for not inviting her mother. The woman who raised her had written a tell-all book in order to cash in on her famous daughter's life. This TV-star FG was well within Fabulous Girl protocol in excluding this badly behaved parent. The wedding day is very tense – why add to it someone who was supposed to give you unconditional love but totally betrayed and abandoned you instead?

Speeches

The idea of speeches is such a nice one: the people who love you get to express their feelings on this special day. Your father welcomes your husband into the family. The best man makes some funny but warm jokes about how thankful he and his pals are that Bingo finally met a girl worth marrying. If only it were possible to guarantee that this was the tone of speeches given at weddings. Alack, alas. Far more common are long speeches without focus that end up insulting at least one person in the room – usually the bride or the groom. It is the responsibility of the wedding MC to read the riot act to speech givers prior to the wedding. Everyone (and really, it should never be more than five speeches, even that is pushing it) should be given a two-minute time limit. They will, of course, exceed this, but you may get lucky and end up with five-minute speeches. A good idea is to schedule a speech between each course of dinner.

What makes a good speech?

1. A Story. But keep it romance related. Tell a brief story about the groom that illustrates what kind of husband he's going to be. Telling a story about what kind of surgeon he is can wait until his retirement dinner, wedding speeches should be about the couple.

2. A Joke. Gentle teasing is an important part of a speech. But the best jokes make fun of either the speech maker or the person he or she is related to. The chief bridesmaid may joke about the bride's kooky fashion sense; the best man may not. The father of the groom may joke about his son's historical ineptitude with women, he may not joke about the *hundreds* that came before.

3. Heart. A toast must include good wishes for the couple. You may know that you're very entertaining and therefore rely on humour to keep the crowd on your side, but you must end on a sentimental note.

4. Brevity. Do not speak for too long. Write this on the top of your notes: 'Keep it short.'

Sex at the Wedding

Sex really should wait until after the wedding reception is over. However, there are a few randy couples out there who just can't hold back. This is especially true for out-of-town weddings where guests and the wedding party are holed up in some quaint inn or cottages. This type of set-up with the romance of true love in the air can inspire French-farce naughtiness. Receptions held at a banquet hall or outdoor garden pose more difficulties, yet it still happens that both guests and the new couple need to sneak off for a bit of cheek.

The bride and groom should opt for a hotel room. But clearly that will only work if their reception is being held in a hotel or inn. Otherwise, you're stuck in the bathroom, and quite frankly, while it may seem indicative of your intense feelings for one another, none of your guests want to happen upon you going at it in a public space. Some level of dignity should be maintained at a wedding.

As a bridesmaid, again, no matter how gorgeous the usher or that tall brute at Table 6 is, you should keep your attention on the job at hand, which is ensuring that the bride is happy. Get the man's number, but don't take this time to go outside for a snog in the back of his car.

However, if you're a guest the rules are a little different. So if you happen to notice that the Table 6 tall brute is looking you over, then feel free to make tonight your special night too. Of course, keep propriety in mind and head for someplace out of the way. Again, the loo seems like the perfect place, but it is at that precise moment that you will encounter the bride or groom and then it will run through the wedding hall like wildfire and the bride will be furious. See 'Scene Stealer' on page 231.

If you happen to walk in on a couple going at it – especially the bride and groom – then mind your own business. Even if that does mean peeing in the next stall with the bride's train covering your feet. Keep it to yourself. Unless of course you walk back into the reception only to discover that the groom is in the room! Then you may need to get the bride alone to ask her if she has lost her mind.

CONFESSING YOUR LOVE FOR THE GROOM

Not the bride, but you have been in love with her future husband for some time? Perhaps you're even the ex, and somehow the bride no longer feels threatened by you. Fooled her? Think again. You are truly the fool if you think that a drunken profession of undying love for Bingo will make him abandon his new bride. If you aren't a couple now, you're not going to be. If you have lust for the man then spill your guts before the wedding day, please.

The surprise Wedding

The perfect compromise for a bride who can't stand all the fuss involved in preparing for a wedding but who couldn't get married without her friends and family present is the surprise wedding. You invite your friends and family to a chic cocktail party – make up some good reason so that they'll really get there and look good – and when they arrive, they find you ready to get hitched (or for some tardy guests, already hitched). This saves you from the endless conversations that plague brides (often with their blessing), detailing every little doily and hors d'oeuvre in the months that precede a wedding. You also remove yourself from the wrangling with relatives over the guest list because you have to do it all yourself. Your immediate family may be cross with you for not allowing them to help you or to have more control over the proceedings, but they will quickly get over it when they have cocktails in their hands and they realize they haven't had to kill themselves helping you organize it all.

Calling off a Wedding at the last minute

You and your parents and he and his parents have all spent a lot of money. The church is booked. Your dress has been altered for the final time. You finally found a photographer who won't make your pictures look dreadful. And it happens. You wake up in the middle of the night with the clear, no-denying-it knowledge that there's no way you can go through with it. He is simply not going to be the last man you sleep with. And when you're really honest with yourself about it, you've had doubts about it since the beginning. You see other couples together and you just know that you don't feel what they do. So. The worst conversation of your life has to happen. You have to tell him. And none of this 'maybe we can just be together and not get married' stuff. This is the end. If you've been engaged to someone and you call it off, the relationship is over. And you have to be prepared that any kind of relationship, even a friendship, will probably be impossible after this. And then you have to make the next worst phone call: to your mother.

All that needs to happen once these two conversations have taken place is to have your mother and maid of honour call around to inform people of your decision. It is best for you, the bride, to remain out of sight for the next few days while you recover. All gifts should be returned to the senders.

Fabulous Girl as Friend of the Bride

SHE'S MAKING A MISTAKE

A friend wants to meet for after-work drinks to tell you some news. Seated at your favourite bar she reveals her surprise: she's getting married! Before you can think through the ramifications you ask, 'Why?' Uh oh. What you really meant was 'Congratulations! You're going to be so happy!' No, actually, what you meant was 'Why?' Your friend and her boyfriend can't make it a week without fighting and wasn't she just telling you about a crush she had on a guy at work? Whatever the circumstances are, your negative reply now hangs between you. You have two choices and very little time to make a move. You can plead surprise yourself and backpeddle like mad. Explain that you were so shocked at her news that you blurted out a ridiculous question. Apologize and congratulate her with as much enthusiasm as you can muster. Or you can make the risky move of plunging in and discussing your concerns. This is difficult for obvious reasons. She's clearly decided to overlook the problems in her relationship and she's hoping everyone else will too. But if you are worried about her future happiness, you can give this a try. Explain that what you want above everything is for her to be happy and that you're just concerned that she hasn't always seemed content in this relationship. Acknowledge that what you're saying is upsetting and that you realize you are risking her friendship in making these statements. And tell her that you hope you're wrong.

Fabulous Girl exception

While the above is the standard FG modus operandi for sticky situations, there are a few notable occasions when you may need to really stick your neck out. If your friend decides during her engagement to have an affair, get pregnant and then pass it off as her fiancé's baby then you should have a more straightforward heart-to-heart. In other words, 'Do you really want to begin a life together on a lie?' Even if she goes ahead and somehow talks herself into being 'mad for her fiancé,' you will at least be satisfied knowing that you tried to shake her into sanity. However, she may turn against you and not want to maintain your friendship. But this type of dishonesty is hardly appealing for the FG, so what's the loss? And if she does allow you to come to the wedding, be sure to firmly grip the pew as the clergyman asks if there is any reason why these two should not be joined in holy matrimony.

BAD GUEST BEHAVIOUR

It happens at most weddings – a terrible gaffe. Usually it is alcohol related. His Aunt Agatha makes a pass at your handsome gay cousin, Ronald. The women under forty realize about halfway through the evening that they've all been felt-up by Fred, an old family friend. All Fabulous Girls should endeavour not only to behave well at a wedding, but to discourage bad behaviour in others. If, for example, you learn that your close friend Patsy is about to drunkenly admit to the bride that she once slept with the groom, you may find it necessary to haul Patsy's ass out of the hall for a good talking to.

WE NEED TO TALK

Naturally, an invitation to a wedding can make even the most poised and happy FG wonder where her life is headed. It can also make her turn into a raving bitch on the day of the wedding. Her perfectly lovely and devoted boyfriend may find himself on the business end of a meltdown. 'You were flirting with that bridesmaid at the engagement party!' 'Where is this going?' You know how it goes. Since this kind of fit is one that you won't see coming, there's little you can do to avoid it. If you feel the undeniable call of the fit coming on, go ahead and get it over with, preferably before you leave for the church. The best plan of all is to avoid any contact with your boyfriend on the day of the wedding. If it's too late – you've already lost it and you haven't even made your morning coffee – then make sure you get some time on your own to chill out before calling a cab to go to the ceremony. If tension with your man does flair up during the reception, you must make an excuse related to your health and leave before actually having a fight.

WHO'S NEXT?

Being at a wedding makes people think of other weddings. Often it makes people think of weddings that have not even happened yet. Like yours. 'When *are* you getting married?' 'So, who's next?' 'What about you and Bingo?' As though if you knew the answer to that question you wouldn't have sent out the invitations by now. Or maybe the answer is 'We're not getting married,' but you really don't feel that someone else's wedding is the place to explain why you don't believe in marriage. The best tactic in this supremely uncomfortable situation is evasion: 'Gosh, I just don't know. How are *you* doing these days?' This last bit should be delivered with intense care expressed through the eyes, hinting that maybe you feel things are not quite okay with your inquisitor. Resist the impulse, which may bubble up, to say, 'I don't know, why don't you ask Bingo?' Remember that people are probably harassing Bingo in the same manner and that you are in this situation together.

SCENE STEALER

You know your friends are happy for you – they've been saying so for the months running up to the wedding, right? So you rightfully expect that on your wedding day they'll be happy for you to be the focus of the celebration. Well, it doesn't always go that way. Some women are so unsettled by the happiness of the bride that they cannot help but interfere with the event. If you find yourself at a wedding and these evil feelings are welling up, you must leave the party. If you can't leave the party you must at least stop drinking. Too much booze could convince you that it's okay to pull the bride into the corner and trap her there while you weep for your own disappointments. Or worse, as one 'friend' of the bride was known to do: loudly announce her own engagement at her friend's wedding reception. Very badly played.

BE A GOOD BRIDESMAID

Being in the bridal party of your close friend or relative is an honour. It is, however, one that is fraught with duty, both financial and emotional. The bridesmaid is usually expected to pay for her bridesmaid gown and accessories. Even though the bride chooses the gown – style and colour – it is the duty of her attendants to cough up the cash. The bride should take into account the various economic levels of her bridal party and ensure that the dress falls into the budget of the brides-maid who earns the least.

Often the bride will present an accessory as a gift to all her attendants. This can be anything from a decorative comb to earrings she'd like them to wear on the day.

A bridesmaid must cheerfully show up at all her fittings. If she is the maid of honour she must throw a shower for the bride-to-be. All bridesmaids should help in shower planning by sending out invitations, deciding on a theme for gifts and so on. A bridesmaid must also attend the rehearsal and, of course, the wedding.

Inevitably, one of the bridesmaids in a bridal party will behave badly. She's thoughtless, she's jealous, whatever. She does not do her duty to the bride. Based on true

FG stories of BBs, here is a list of activities to avoid:

1. Being late for the rehearsal and/or the wedding. This will naturally drive the bride out of her mind.

2. Refusing to sit at the head table because you can't be separated from your boyfriend for two hours. Or insisting that your boyfriend who is not in the bridal party sit at the head table.

3. Not noticing that the bride needs you to go to the washroom with her to help take her veil off for the second half of the evening. Particularly if you're not noticing because you're trying to shag one of the ushers.

4. Telling the bride that the hairdresser has made her look like a character from Star Trek. If you really think her hair or makeup looks terrible, you must let her know – but be gentle and supportive. 'I think it will be perfect if you just switch the blue eyeshadow to taupe!'

5. Complaining. About the dress, the shoes, the hair, the cost. Keep it to yourself.

GIFTS

Wedding Lists

Despite the wedding list's inherent vulgarity, it can be useful if you don't know the couple's taste or needs well. Using the list is not a breach of etiquette since you are only trying to please the happy, greedy couple.

How much?

The conventional reasoning is that you should spend about as much as your hosts will be spending on the food and drink. The Fabulous Girl, however, knows that she is free to spend as much or as little as she can afford. If you're a student, no one expects you to spend as much as the bride's doting and wealthy uncle. And don't fall into the trap of feeling you have to spend more on a gift if the wedding is going to be formal.

Timing

Although it's nice to have your gift all wrapped up and ready to go by the day of the wedding, you really have a full year to send a gift. If the gift you really want to give has to be delivered after the festivities, send a card to the bride and groom with your best wishes, saying a gift will follow.

Money

Generally, money does not show the same thoughtfulness as a gift. However, you can give money as a wedding gift, particularly if the couple is young.

Group Gifts

It's perfectly acceptable to go in on a gift with a group of friends. If, for example, you know that your friend and her fiancé won't be able to afford a honeymoon without some financial assistance, it's nice to round up some friends to contribute together.

Taste

Don't go out on a limb, particularly when it comes to decorative gifts. Better to give a boring but practical set of steel mixing bowls than a nice-if-you-like-that-kind-of-thing garden ornament.

Second Marriages

HAVE A SECOND MARRIAGE WITH STYLE

You've been through it once. You spent the money, wore the big, stupid dress, had it all come unravelled. This time – hopefully – you're more focused on the partnership that you're entering and less on the pomp of the actual wedding. Besides, you've also got better things to do with your money now – mortgage payments, investments, private-school fees and so on. Which means you can actually have a nicer wedding this time. Your mother can't force you into a terrible dress. You can't be bullied by his mother into having more guests than you want. You can now just throw a very chic, small affair – something like a very festive cocktail party – to celebrate your wedding.

And do not wear white. Keep your ensemble to other hues. Think pewter, sand, even off-white if you must, but truly, anything too virginal becomes laughable.

BECOMING THE NOT-SO-EVIL STEPMOTHER

You've gone and fallen in love with a man who has children, either from a previous marriage or a one-night stand, it doesn't matter. He's committed for life, and if you say yes to his proposal, so are you. It doesn't really matter if his kids are brats or little angels, you have to decide if you can truly handle being a stepmother.

Top ten things to consider before saying 'I do'
1. Age. How old are the kids? If they are quite young, then you will have some influence over their upbringing. If they are teens, then most of the raising has been done and you will have to cope with whatever kind of behaviour is already

established in them.

2. Money. You may not think his child-support cheques and his financing of his kids' college educations will bother you. Just wait until you can't go on holiday because he has to cough up cash for a French tutor.

3. Time. Will they be living with you? Will it be only every other weekend? Really think about how much of a life change this will be.

4. Phones, Internet and Television. As the kids grow, your access to your own electronics may be hampered. You may need to think about a separate phone line and about having to adjust your television watching to include horror films, sci-fi and cartoons.

5. Mess. Kids are messy. Maybe you are too. How do you feel about picking up after them?

6. Delinquency. You think Billy's trouble with the law is a one-time offence? Wasn't there a twenty in your wallet this morning? And how do you feel about having the police come to your door at 3 A.M.?

7. Sex. Yours and theirs. Kids will cramp your sex life when they're in your home. If they're older, will you be able to cope with those 'unofficial sleepovers'? Will your husband? Are you going to be running interference?

8. The Posse. If you live close to the kids' mum's house, chances are your place may also become a drop-in centre for the kids and their friends. Add this point to the mess factor.

9. Her. What is the relationship between your future husband and his ex-wife? Will she be calling you or criticizing you on how you co-raise her kids? Can you handle this?

10. Him. How is your future husband with his kids? Does he have control over them? Are they left to run wild? Do you and he have similar outlooks on how kids should be raised? Will he let you have a say in how *his* kids are raised?

All of the above

If you choose to have kids of your own at some point, then you will probably wave aside all of these points as being just the way kids are. But when someone else's children are suddenly thrust upon you, you may find that the resentment and frustration are not what you bargained for.

The FG stepmum

So despite all of the above, or because of it, you're going through with the marriage anyway. And you know what that makes you? That's right: Stepmum. If you think that the relationship with his kids will immediately get better once you're married, think again. If the kiddies are little tykes this transition will be smoother. After all, what the hell does a two-year-old know? But if you're marrying an older gent who has preteens and teens, then look out. Just like those pop quizzes in high school, you will be tested. If your husband doesn't have full custody, then chances are you only have the little dears every other weekend or on holidays.

As the new stepmum, you are inheriting whatever type of relationship they have with their father. If they're quiet and sullen with him, don't expect it to be any different with you unless you are prepared to really work at it. However, unlike simply dating their dad, as a stepmother you now have more say in how they behave in your home. If they seem to consider weekends at Dad's a vacation where the adults cook, clean and basically entertain them, then you may have to make them understand that they are part of a family. And that means they have to do their part.

Divorce

LEAVING YOUR HUSBAND

If as a married FG you've finally decided that your marriage is over, the most difficult part may be having to say it out loud. Tell your closest friends first, before even telling your parents, for if Mum and Dad are still married they may not take it well, or if they too are divorced they may gloat or quip, 'You're just like me.' None of which you want to hear. Girlfriends, however, will provide the necessary comfort zone.

As the Fabulous Girl friend, you are probably aware that your best pal is going to sit down with hubby to tell him she's leaving. Stay by the phone. When she calls, offer to come over or invite her to your place. Either way, show up and be there if she needs you.

If the FG is in fact the one who is left by her hubby, then the whole separation process will be a shock. Again, be there immediately and let her cry and rant. Don't give too many opinions - 'He's a rat that's never deserved you' – as your friend may turn her anger against you, for she may be blaming herself.

IS IT POLITE TO SUE FOR ALIMONY?

There are laws that define how money and assets shall be divided once a couple separates and then divorces. But does that mean that an FG should take advantage of every chance she has to access her ex's bank account? If the two of you had children, then their welfare should be the primary concern of you both. Any hesitation on his part to meet his financial obligations to your children should be dealt with seriously. But what if you didn't have children? Did you put your career on hold to support him while he went through medical school? Did you alter your ambitions to follow him from one city to another for his career? Anything of this nature surely has had a financial effect on you, now and possibly into the future. You made these sacrifices thinking the two of you would be together forever and that whatever wealth came out of your mutual plans would be shared. It's fair then to expect some support from him after your split. If, however, the two of you were on an equal footing, you both worked during the time of your marriage, then it's harder to rationalize his owing you money after the marriage ends.

The signing of the papers

This is the Fabulous Girl's Declaration of Independence – a sad ritual in which the FG must take pen in hand and sign the divorce papers. But sign them she must, and then it's all over but the crying, shouting and perhaps cheering. An FG should not go through this day alone. Invite a friend along with you to the lawyer's office. Then go out for a cocktail.

Fabulous Girls must rally around their divorcing friends. Take them out for the night and don't talk about the divorce unless they want to. But be prepared for tears. Signing the papers may be the first time it hits your friend that her marriage is over. The second time will be when she receives her copy in the post. Both of these occasions are yucky and will require you as the friend to offer up a shoulder and perhaps some scotch or martinis.

Bad-mouthing the ex in front of the kids

As tempting as it is, young mums and young stepmums should not under any circumstances vent their frustrations about exes in front of the offspring. No matter how tempting it is to say to little Timmy, 'Your father is just too cheap to send you to private school – he's single-handedly denying you a proper education,' don't say it! Likewise for the stepmum: the ex-wife may be a total bitch who is never polite to you or your husband, but sending her not-so-subtle messages via the kids is unfabulous. Not to mention cruel to the kids.

Once our dance was finished, I told Nice that I was going to the bar to get us some more champagne. Lucy, one of the bridesmaids, was also at the bar. I was asking her about her gorgeous unbridal-party-like dress when she suddenly let out a squeal.

We both turned and saw the grey-bearded man Eleanor had been dancing with earlier, now standing beside Lucy. He had his hand on her butt and was giving it a mighty squeeze. Poor Lucy was mortified, but the grey-bearded groper just grinned and waltzed off.

'Who is that guy?' I whispered to Lucy.

'I don't know, but I feel like I need a shower now.'

Instead, we went to the ladies' room, me carrying both glasses of champagne. There we found Missy, Eleanor and Helen, who was looking quite distraught.

'My Uncle Jack is going around grabbing women's bottoms!' cried Helen.

'Yes, he certainly is,' said Lucy.

'Oh, God, I'm so sorry. I don't know what to do, he's always been a bit loopy but . . .'

Lucy put her arm around Helen and said, 'Please don't worry, it's not your fault. It's a beautiful wedding, and one bad thing always has to happen, so now you can forget about worrying for the rest of the evening. Come on, let's go dance with our husbands.'

And off they went.

I asked Missy why she and Joe were fighting, and she shrugged. 'It's like he doesn't trust me anymore.'

'What makes you think he doesn't trust you?' I asked.

'Um. Well, he read an e-mail I wrote to you guys about wanting to do it with Francis.' Missy started chewing on a fingernail but Eleanor swatted her hand away.

'He read your e-mail! That is grounds for divorce. How dare he invade your privacy that way. How did he see it, anyway?' Eleanor stood with her hands on her hips.

Missy explained that she'd left her laptop on and her e-mail program running one afternoon when she left for the gym. When she'd come home, she'd found Joe crying on the sofa.

'I couldn't even get mad at him for snooping. I mean, obviously I've been making him feel insecure or he wouldn't have been looking,' said Missy.

Eleanor still didn't look convinced by this argument.

'Come on, El, it's not like all of us haven't done a little snooping over the years,' I said. Then I turned to Missy. 'So what's going on now?'

'He's asked for a trial separation. Can I stay at your place for a bit? I don't want to be alone right now.'

CHAPTER EIGHT

Home and Family

It's really not that Missy is impossible to live with. In many ways she is an ideal roommate. She's tidy, she's quiet, she bakes cookies. But very quickly it became obvious that my apartment was not big enough for the two of us. I'd be trying to rush out the door to a waiting taxi when I'd realize that my keys were not in their normal home by the coat rack.

'Oh, keys don't go there anymore. They hang on this little rack here by the fridge.' Missy smiled proudly.

Once the towels and sheets had moved, the kitchen had been entirely rearranged and all the furniture in the living room had been spun around, I called an estate agent. Although I was putting off telling Nice, I told Missy and Eleanor over one of our dinners at Dominick's.

'You may as well do it on your own, that's how we all end up anyway,' said Eleanor darkly. As she neared the end of her pregnancy, Eleanor was becoming more and more ominous. Missy and I had started to joke that we weren't going to make it through nine months.

'Missy, I know you were feeling like you weren't ready to be alone yet. I don't want you to think that I'm abandoning you. I could help you find a new roommate if you want.'

'I'm fine. I don't want a flat mate, actually. Can I just keep your flat?' asked Missy.

You see a lot of terrible places when you start looking. I

went home crying after a couple of trips out. So many of the places I looked at were small and dark, and I began to panic that I'd never be able to afford something that felt like home. I'd go back to my apartment and think, why am I going to spend all the money I have to live in something that isn't nearly as nice as this? Then I'd trip across some new furniture project that Missy had dragged home with her and resolve again to find my own place. Betty, my estate agent, kept telling me to relax, that eventually we'd find just the right thing for me. I loved her being about as far removed from a stereotypical real estate agent as you could imagine. She was pretty and stylish, and we were always bumping into each other at vintage boutiques.

She called me at work on a Thursday about a place.

'I'm on deadline, I can't leave the office right now. Can we go and see it tomorrow?'

'Mmm. I think you need to find a way to see this place today. Like, right now. It's in *the* building. Oh, hang on a minute, I'm going through a tunnel. If I cut out, I'll call you back.'

She did cut out. Which gave me a second to think of my favourite building in the city. It's a small building on a side street. Originally, it had been a college but it had been converted about five years earlier into luxury flats. I had once gone to a party in one and had fallen in love with the place. I'd told Betty in our first meeting that it was where I really wanted to live. She'd laughed and said that things rarely came up there and to try to keep an open mind about what my future home might look like. I decided not to mention to anyone at work where I was slipping off to.

Betty called back to say that she was downstairs and to come on down. I ran.

'It's my place. I feel like the guys who are in there just need to get out so I can move in. I can already see all my furniture there. I'm going to paint the big living-room wall lavender. And having the deck is going to feel like another room all summer,' I gushed over dinner with Nice. He seemed to be taking it all in his stride. He was nodding and smiling.

'It does sound great. But you'll need to see a lot of places before you know if this is really what you want to do.'

'Um. Well, actually, I have been looking,' I said. Nice started to frown. 'I've seen about a dozen places and they've all been terrible. This just feels so right to me. It's what I want.'

'This is what you want?' Nice was looking down into his drink. 'I can't believe you didn't tell me you were looking.'

'I guess I was worried about how it might make you feel. But it just feels like my home. I'm going to make an offer.'

Now Nice was just nodding. 'All right then.'

I started to get worried. I mean, I'd thought that this was kind of a big step to take on my own, but I hadn't thought that other people would have a problem with it, even if one of those people was my boyfriend. I should have told him earlier, but every time I'd started to I'd gotten scared that he would take it badly. Sitting across from Nice, I realized I'd made a huge mistake and that all I could do was damage control.

'I can't wait for you to see it. I think you're really going to love it.'

Nice shook his head. 'I don't think so. This isn't going to work. You want to move ahead on your own. I'm ready for us to move forward together. We just don't want the same things.'

'What are you saying? That if I won't get a place with you we're breaking up?' My voice was starting to crack. 'I know I should have talked this over with you. That was really stupid. But you know there's room for someone to move in eventually . . .'

'Someone?'

'Well, I mean you. There's room for you to move in if that's what we want to do.'

Nice reached for his wallet and threw some money on the table.

'It's obviously not what you want to do. Good luck with your new place.'

Home Sweet Home

As an FG moves through life, with all the demands of career and relationships that usually go with it, she appreciates her nest more and more. It can be her sanctuary, her source of inspiration or a reflection of her creativity. Her relationship to her home – be it a rental or her own – may also be complicated. Making a commitment to home and family is decidedly in the realm of grown-ups. And although the FG is a grown-up, she may occasionally have mixed feelings about her place in this world.

BUYING ON YOUR OWN

You've finally saved enough money to think about buying your own place. You phone the bank or a mortgage broker and lo and behold – they're going to give little old you a mortgage. You're elated! And so proud of yourself. You call to give friends and family the news, thinking they will be as thrilled as you are. Naturally, then, you're shocked when instead of hearing delight in their voices you hear – what's that? – sympathy? You've saved 45K for a downpayment, and they feel sorry for you. And you know why.

Going ahead and making this move on your own (particularly if you have a boyfriend) is like admitting defeat for some (okay, lots of) people. Instead of asking you what kind of place you're going to be looking for your mother wants to know what the rush is. Your work-mates want to know what *his* hold up is. And, of course, if any of these feelings coincide with a bit of hesitation you might naturally be feeling yourself, these conversations can be devastating. Be tough. Be firm and repetitive if necessary about what a good thing this is that you're doing. And remind yourself that you can sell a house as easily as you can buy one (markets willing) if you ever decide you want to cohabit. And go out for drinks to celebrate with your more sensible friends.

HOUSEWARMING YOURSELF

You've done it – you've saved up enough money for the down payment, you've jumped through enough hoops to make the bank happy and you bought a house all on your own. Naturally you want to show off your new house or flat – and your accomplishment – to your friends and family. This is an enormous rite of passage for you. FGs who make this move solo will often feel like they are being left out of the gift loop. For traditional women there is a seemingly never-ending opportunity to be given. Get engaged – an engagement party and lots of presents for you and your fiancé! Get married eight months later? The skies open and down come blenders, crystal wine decanters, 300-thread-count sheets, not to mention that cheque from Uncle Harold to help you out with your first house. First house? More presents of course. Have a baby? Get ready for more Snugglis and intellect-stimulating toys than you'll know what to do with. If you step off this road it can feel like you become gift-invisible, which may strike an FG as unfair. Why isn't she being praised – and showered with presents – for looking after herself?

If you throw yourself a party when you buy a place, don't expect everyone to bring you presents. You must invite people to see your place, but you must be offering *them* something: your hospitality. And isn't that one of the reasons you got your own place – to have a great place to entertain? Invite people over and proudly give them a tour of your new digs. Offer them cocktails and snacks like the grown-up that you are. Of course, when people aren't expected to shell out for gifts they often feel more generous than when they are.

PEOPLE: PLUMBER, HANDYMAN, CLEANING LADY

Once you become a home or flat owner, you're going to need some new people in your life. An FG can't be good at everything. Owning a place is not going to endow you with sudden knowledge of electrical circuitry or the widths of copper pipes. Luckily there are scores of those who do know these things, and you can employ them. The FG does not subscribe to the Zen of Motorcycle Maintenance. Many FGs believe their time is better spent making money or just making dinner reservations than it is learning how to re-wire her living room. However, as unusual as it may seem, there may come a point when the FG-as-DIY-girl rears her head. Perhaps it's a desire for full-on independence, or simply that she loves the feel of that power tool vibrating in her hand. But just in case the do-it-herself project doesn't quite work, or the deadline for her cocktail party is looming then it is wise to have on hand the phone numbers for the following:

- A plumber
- An electrician
- A handyman
- A cleaning lady. (Of course, if you can afford it, it's nice to have a standing appointment with a cleaning lady. But even if this isn't in your cards just yet, it's nice to know one you trust to call upon before a party or a visit from your parents.)

An FG can often find that she needs help making her life run. Having someone clean her house or flat is one of the best timer savers she can invest in. Having probably done nasty jobs herself at one time or another, she may feel a little uncomfortable hiring such a person. Hiring an independent cleaning lady rather than one through an agency is a good idea. That way you know all the money you're paying her goes to her rather than to the agency taking a cut. Many people who would never dream of being rude to a waiter – and there are plenty who would – for some reason feel that cleaning ladies do not warrant polite treatment. By hiring a cleaning person you are entering into quite an intimate relationship with someone. You should offer her a coffee if you're having one and discuss with her what is more comfortable for both of you – your leaving her alone while she works, or your hanging around.

NEIGHBOURS

When you think of your home – be it house or flat you probably think of the space you actually own or inhabit. But the space that affects you is actually much larger than that. There is the street outside your home, the hallways of your building, the garden . . . and then there are the walls that separate you from them – *them* being the neighbours. Even if you have a cordial relationship with your neighbours things can get sticky. As one FG discovered, the walls that separate your bedroom from your neighbour's may not stop any sounds from making the trip over. If your bedtime is now fraught with worry over whether tonight is going to be a lucky one for Sally next door because she and her boyfriend like to scream embarrassingly clichéd phrases, you need to politely let them know. No, not with a handwritten note, but with song. The next time you start to hear the sounds of love making their way through the walls, burst into song, just loud enough (and you should know roughly what decibel level) for Sally and Mr You're-So-Hot to hear you.

Of course, sexually active neighbours are not the sole cause of noise pollution. The Fabulous Girl knows never to play music outdoors or to have an intimate chat at 2 A.M.

on the front lawn (sound carries in the quiet night).

But for the FG, especially if she works at home or needs to get some rest on the weekends, her neighbours' endless screaming or blaring radios can completely ruin her day. The Fabulous Girl gets tough in these situations.

Yes, she might create some tension by doing so. But she's not trying to win a popularity contest, she's trying to enjoy her living space. Starting with her immediate neighbours, she goes over and introduces herself and lets them know that she works at home, or that she'd really appreciate it if they wouldn't start their chainsaw experiment until at least 10 A.M. on the weekends.

Family

You want a baby

It can come over you unexpectedly, the desire to have a baby. Yesterday your biggest preoccupation was getting through all the work on your desk while still finding a moment to run out and get a facial. But today you can't keep your mind from turning to a more primal desire: you want to get pregnant. If you're in a relationship with someone who is as keen to pro-create as you are, then you're off to the races. You are probably going to tell a few close girlfriends, and maybe your mother, that you've made this decision. But you should con-sider not telling many people, or even those very close to you. You don't know how long it's going to take you to get pregnant or, sad to say, if you will at all. Many FGs put off the baby phase of their life as long as they can, hoping to achieve the career goals they're after before taking a break from the workplace. While this is a perfectly understandable impulse, it's one that can make getting pregnant that much tougher.

The last thing you need is for every conversation to start with, 'So . . . ?' What you may *not* do is announce at cocktail parties, that you and your man are 'trying.' (And you really, really mustn't make the quote mark signs with your hands while saying 'trying.' Just never make the quote mark signs with your hands, ever.) Because when you say you are 'trying,' what you are really saying is that you are having sex, and why do you need to proclaim that in a party situation?

Sneak-A-Baby

An FG wants it all: great career, great apartment, great guy, great baby! Oops. Being the busy overachiever that she is, the FG has probably put off gooey thoughts of herself at home with a cashmere bundle cooing in a crib. But whether she has anticipated it or not, the desire for a baby may strike. She will have to do some serious rearranging, to make room for a child. Her sense of herself is going to have to undergo some renovations as well. She will no longer be the happy-go-lucky girl who can go out to a party on a moment's notice (unless she has a wonderful live-in nanny). She also has to convince the man in her life that this is the right moment for them to move from couple to parents.

And she must really do this – not present her pregnancy to him as a done deal. It's amazing how many women who did anything it took to *not* get pregnant throughout their twenties and early thirties are somehow caught off guard by birth-control issues in their mid- to late thirties. Women who have been on the Pill for years suddenly find themselves pregnant. Maybe they have an unspoken pact with their men that this is the only way they're going to do it – by 'accident.' Maybe they're crazy. It is both unethical and risky to try the Sneak-a-Baby route to motherhood. You may think he's a stand-up guy who will stick with you through this, but you don't know for sure. You also risk his resenting you, which could happen even if he falls deliriously in love with the baby.

Having a baby on your own, or Plan B

If you are ready for a child in every other way except being in a relationship, then you may consider going it alone. Many FGs have what is known as a Plan B: a way to get pregnant that does not involve a romantic commitment from a man. This is tricky to pull off – tricky but not impossible. Some Plan B's involve gay friends. An FG may have a gay friend who is willing to knock her up (in some way or other). The FG may also have a male friend who is not a romantic possibility but who is willing to do the job. For reasons which are obvious, everyone involved in these scenarios must be very clear about what they are doing.

If you do decide to go ahead with a Plan B, you need a lawyer. You obviously need to have a frank conversation with your potential donor, but you still need a lawyer. How involved is this man going to be in the future of your child? What are you going to do when your child wants to know who her daddy is? What if he goes on to have more children in the more traditional way? What if you do? Is money going to change hands?

YOU DON'T WANT A BABY

Choosing to remain child-free can be a difficult choice for some, or not a choice at all for others. We're not discussing women who for whatever biological reason cannot have a baby, but those who choose not to even try. This decision is often very threatening to other people in our society. They will say to your face that you are selfish and shallow. Well, maybe you are. You want a life that is free for travel and adventure. You may not want to put your body through the trauma. You want to work hard to pay for Prada heels, not a pram. Instead of saving for a college tuition, you're saving for a winter house in St Barts.

Be prepared that if you remark to a roomful of people that you don't plan on having kids, more often than not someone will ask you why. Usually these people are parents. They may be resentful that you are not choosing the common path. They think that you are somehow being critical of them by not doing the normal thing. Take a deep breath, and tell the truth: 'I'm not interested, I like my freedom.'

The phrase 'child-free' was coined by people who chose not to have children but resented the incompleteness suggested by the term 'childless.' Of course 'child-free' is a source of much anger for parents, as they feel the term implies that they have lost their freedom by having kids, or that they are somehow imprisoned by their choice. Well, actually, by and large they are. Parents have lost their freedom to move about the world as they did when they were without the kids. But they obviously made the choice to have kids, and one would think they are happy to relinquish some of those freedoms. Nonetheless, it may be better to refrain from using the term 'child-free' around newer parents of your own age group who are probably grappling with their decision or adjusting to their new way of life.

Of course, if you are around a new mum who can't stop talking about her 'spawn' and bugging you to have one, then the term 'child-free' becomes very, very useful and should be employed. Consider the term to be in the FG arsenal of conversational controls.

WHEN YOU MEET SOMEONE WHO IS PREGNANT

When a colleague or someone you've simply been introduced to at a dinner party tells you she's pregnant, you know to express pleasure in her news. If you are of a baby-bearing age yourself, her confession may trip off other feelings as well which are better kept to yourself. If you haven't yet had a child, or aren't sure if you are going to, try not to use this moment to air all your baby-related anxieties. You must be very close friends indeed to ask a woman how she and her man will deal with a declining sex drive in those first baby years. Do not ask her what the odds are that her baby may have congenital defects because of her age. Don't linger on the subject of the difficulties of blending the modes of motherhood and career. And don't go on and on about how you would never raise a child in the city as she plans to do. Rest assured that these are all issues that keep her up in the middle of the night. She does not need you to tell her how frightening having a baby can be.

NAMES

When chatting with parents-to-be, it is common for people to enquire after the list of potential names that are currently in play. Whatever names they mention your response should be the same: 'Oh, that's nice.' That is all that is required of you. No one is asking you what you would name *your* child or even what you think of their choice. Do not, as happens with shocking regularity, start a monologue about how you knew a Linda and whoa, what a bitch! If they want your opinion they will ask for it. Learn to distinguish between what is being told to you, 'I'm naming him Mark' versus 'What do you think of the name Mark?'

Of course, if your friend or relative is naming her child Dweedleduff or something truly crazy, then you may casually ask the origins of the name and if perhaps he or she has thought through the culture in which the child will be raised and therefore whether it is an appropriate choice.

These rules must be applied even more stringently to

babies who are already born and named. FGs have been known to be screamed at by horrified relatives after making the call from the hospital. Having just endured the emotional and physical trauma that is childbirth, the last thing an FG needs is to be criticized in any way. She certainly doesn't need to be asked, 'What kind of name is Isabel? That's a terrible name! Why don't you give her a nice name like Mary, not an awful name like Isabel?' With the FG reduced to tears and the baby reduced to Mary, the only happy person is the FG's mother, although slightly annoyed when the FG's three-year-old daughter can't stop calling the baby Mary-not-Isabel.

TEACHING CHILDREN MANNERS

One of the most important lessons to teach your children is how to move through society with ease and grace. The child-rearing principles of the last few decades have been focused on fulfilling the child's creativity and self-confidence. Obviously these things are important, but if they are emphasized to the detriment of other, more co-operative values you are doing your child a grave disservice. Kids (and adults, for that matter) who cannot share, who do not know the value in thinking of other peoples' feelings, are not well liked and have trouble getting ahead in the world. Example is the best way to teach children the importance of manners. Particularly vital is how you treat them. Many people have a distinct set of rules for their own children, and it's often not nearly as decorous as it is for the rest of the world.

WHEN PEOPLE TELL YOU WHAT TO DO WITH YOUR KIDS

Everyone has a sense of what child-rearing should look like. Usually this is based on their own experience of childhood. Either they feel like their upbringing was correct and so everyone should raise their children in a similar fashion or they feel like they were raised wrongly and so everyone should do the opposite. In any case, no role in the world is as commented upon as that of the mother. Everyone's an expert. And many will not hesitate to tell a woman what she should be doing with her child.

This is both upsetting and annoying. The FG wants to do this job well and is susceptible to the hints that she is doing otherwise. We're not talking about the helpful, supportive conversations that can exist between parents – 'Have you read this excellent book on getting them to sleep through the night?' – we're talking about people who jam a dummy in your baby's mouth after you've told them you've decided not to use one. It's true that if you are firm and clear with people in these moments they may think you're a bit of a bitch. But they will also stop sticking a dummy in your baby's mouth.

When the baby cries

You feel bad, the baby obviously feels bad, everyone who is staring at you in the mall feels bad. Your baby is crying. No, make that keening, and you know there's nothing you can do about it until you get to the car, bathroom or wherever. Meanwhile, people are staring at you like they're ready to call the NSPCC. You do not need to give apologetic looks to anyone who is staring at you, and you may brush off any questions after your baby's health. There's very little you can do. Other than leave the situation.

The movies
Unless you are at one of those screenings reserved for parents and babies, you must leave if your little one fusses for more than a couple of minutes. Actually, even if you *are* at one of those screenings you should get up if the baby screams for

too long. No one in the cinema has paid to listen to your child express his teething pain.

A restaurant

If you are in a posh place, you should probably have already booked a babysitter. It's an excellent idea to introduce small children to the culture of restaurants. The more you do the better behaved they will be. But there are restaurants that are better suited for children than others. You're not banished to fast food just because you're in the family way, but it is a good idea to go to laid-back places *en famille*. Even in a relaxed spot, you must get up and go outside if your baby takes a fit. A little crying or hollering is fine, but you know very well when your child is about to go over to the other side. Step outside, walk around the block, see if you can shake it off and then come back. It's just not fair to the other people in the restaurant otherwise.

The plane

This is one of the toughest situations for parents. There's just nowhere to go, and frankly, who can blame the kid for crying – commercial air travel sucks these days. The food, the seat size – you'd cry too if it were more acceptable. Talk to your paediatrician before your trip. If you're travelling with an infant it's probably a good idea to nurse or give the baby a bottle during takeoff and landing to ease the pressure in his ears. Some doctors recommend giving babies or small children a dose of pain relief to make them sleepy for the duration of the flight. If all else fails and the baby cannot be comforted, there's nothing you can do. And you don't owe anyone an apology. Of course it's miserable for everyone, but what can you do?

A DEATH IN THE FAMILY

Because an FG is such a responsible, caring person, it's likely that when someone in her family dies, many of the burdens of planning a funeral will fall on her. If she was close to the person who died, this may actually be a blessing in disguise. Having the tasks surrounding a funeral to look after can be distracting and even comforting. If she comes from a religious family, what needs to be done will be obvious to her. If your family is not associated with a church or synagogue, things are slightly harder to manage. The staff of a funeral home will help with many of the plans. She should organize some kind of get-together for family. An afternoon event makes sense if people with children will be attending.

How to help your friend during the grieving process
The Fabulous Girl can come to the aid of her closest friends during their time of need. The death of a parent or other loved one is always a shock no matter how prepared one is. If you receive the phone call from your friend, immediately offer your services:

1. Make telephone calls to mutual friends and let her employers know.

2. If she's single with little family, offer to escort her to the various funeral homes or dial them up and get quotes on packages.

3. Help arrange the service and any reception afterwards.

4. Offer to have her stay with you, or you with her, for at the very least the night of the funeral.

HOW TO END FAMILY FEUDS

The worst kind of family feud is the kind your inherit. You're not even sure why you don't like your cousins on your mother's side, but you don't. The mere mention of them at family dinners spurs everyone to repeat the three irritating qualities they are known to embody. After a while it doesn't make sense to you. You've never met these people. You're not sure why they've been shut out. In fact, the feud likely has its origins in some generation before yours. It takes courage to break out of these family structures.

So when you receive a call from that 'other' cousin who was – according to family lore – a no-good, you hesitate briefly before accepting his invitation to dinner. Sure, you've never had any first-hand experience with him, but such terrible stories couldn't be all conjecture. Off you go to dinner, anticipating much discomfort. Only it doesn't unfold that way. To your surprise, your cousin is gracious, kind and open. It turned out that neither of you knows what started the family feud – which you rename the 'family fuss.' After some wine and laughs, you two cousins decide to remain close and ignore the crap you've inherited from both sets of parents. But you will definitely be upsetting people if you rock the boat by hanging out. You may need to warn those who may feel slighted by your actions.

If you're the one who wants to patch it up, start small. Send a letter to your long-lost cousin or whomever and introduce the idea of a reconciliation.

WHEN TO CUT THINGS OFF WITH YOUR FAMILY

Sometimes there's just no way to resolve family disputes. You've tried to work it out with your parents. But your folks hate your common-law boyfriend and flatly refuse to include him in family functions or even to acknowledge him when you're together. You've told your brother you can't bail him out of debt again. It's time – at least for now – to take a break from being disappointed. If it's at all possible you should tell the offending family member what your plans are. Let your brother know that until he at least starts making an effort to repay his debt to you, you won't be able to have any contact with him. You're looking forward to that changing, but until he stops gambling, there's just no other way. Try to make these announcements in as calm a way as possible. If you scream them out during one of your regular scraps with your stepmother, they will be lost in your usual fight-and-make-up pattern. To really cut people off you must be calm and firm in your communication. You have to let them know that this is an exceptional thing you're saying. You need them to hear that you've set a limit and you expect them to honour it. Of course, at first they won't. They will try and drag you back into the old dysfunctional way you always operated in.

THE FAMILY FUCK-UP

Every family has one: the person who seems to channel the entire family's worth of trouble and project it out into the world in spectacular ways. Your younger sister who went from smoking joints at recess to getting pregnant by her drug dealer to engaging in petty crime herself. Your father's devastating problem with gambling and what it's done to your mother's future security. Your cousin's coke addiction which she won't have treated, leaving her parents waiting for the phone calls which come randomly from around the country. When dealing with family fuck-ups, an FG needs to bring all her diplomatic abilities to the fore.

The problem with fuck-ups is that they tend to work in secrecy. If you are close to them, they will want to draw you into a web of secrecy as well. The FG should avoid this at all costs. Not only does it compromise her relationships with the rest of her family, it does not help the fuck-up either. Your knocked-up little sister may confide in you and then ask you to keep her secrets from your parents. Your father may rely on all his children to not call a spade a spade – a gambler a gambler – to keep up his dangerous habits. Be clear that you can't make any such promises and that you don't like being put in such a position. You can still be available to help this person but not necessarily in the way he or she wants help. When the late night-call comes – it's always the late-night call, isn't it? – asking for money or for a place to stay, make an offer that you feel will really help. Your sister can stay with you for a month and the two of you will make it a project to find her a place of her own that she can afford. You'll phone around and look into treatment centres for your cousin. You'll be a help but not the solution to their problems.

MOVING HOME FOR THE SECOND TIME

Despite the FG's best efforts, there may come a time, usually in her mid-twenties (or after a divorce at any age), when she will need to bunk out at home – 'Home' not meaning that groovy flat you rented when you had that groovy job but the one you moved out of after high school or college. That's right, Mum and Dad's. This is a most difficult transition. For many young people, just when they've gained some respect from their parents and proven themselves as adults, disaster strikes and renders them teens again. Depending on the type of relationship you have with your folks, this can be a positive retreat to help regain composure or it can be hell in a bunk bed.

The Conversation

It's humiliating to have to make the first phone call asking if you can come home. A few tears may elicit sympathy, but what you need to do is sit down with your folks and tell it like it is. Ask them what their expectations are while you're staying there. It's not a hotel, and you need to know what will make them comfortable. Remind them that you are not a teen any longer and will not adhere to curfews. You're not going to be updating them on the hour as to your whereabouts. Let them know you may sometimes opt to sleep at a friend's or your boyfriend's.

Meals

If your mum is in any way domestic, or if she isn't, she may see this as the time to be the perfect mum you never had. She may start doing your laundry, cooking meals for you and cleaning up after you. For the first week or two this is fine – after all, some sort of drama must have forced you home, so a bit of TLC from Mum is just what you need. But after two weeks, it's time to pick up the slack and do your share around the house. Cook for your parents and help with the chores.

Calling

Because your folks do worry about you. If you're not coming home for a meal or don't plan to sleep at home, call them or leave a note before you go out.

Bills and board

If you really are financially strapped, then paying board may be difficult, but you shouldn't take your folks for a free ride either. Two months or enough to save up for another apartment is plenty. More than that and you are a sponger. Discuss in advance what you all feel is fair. Even if your parents don't need your contribution, you may feel more comfortable about your stay if you make it anyway. Paying your share of the phone and utilities is the minimum gesture you should make.

A little loan

Things may be even tighter than that. You may need to borrow money from your parents as well as stay with them for a while. Again, be frank. Let them know that you intend to pay it back and propose a schedule for payments. You're going to have to live frugally if you decide to go this route. If you don't want them thinking you are just freeloading, you can't come home with designer shopping bags once a week.

The getaway plan

You may not know how long it will take to get back on your feet, but try to set a goal and tell it to your parents: 'I only need three months.' If it turns out you need longer, then address it at that time. Don't let yourself fall into the trap of having time just pass you by.

Sex

If your parents let you do it in your room in high school, then you may think it's all fine and dandy now. But really, there is something rather pathetic about bonking your boyfriend in your parents' room if you're over the age of nineteen.

A MEMBER OF YOUR FAMILY MOVES IN WITH YOU

You hope it's temporary. At least that's what your sister Joan says when she shows up out of work and evicted. But you know Joan. You grew up with Joan. Joan won't leave until she meets another man to sponge off. But, for now, you're the one she turns to. You must lay down some ground rules. First and foremost is money. If she's staying longer than a month, she needs to contribute to the rent. If less than a month, she must cough up for groceries and long-distance calls. What do you do, however, if Joan just won't pay?

The FG may have to adopt the 'it takes two' approach to

life. As in 'It takes two to keep two.' So when you run out of toilet paper, don't replace it (keep a secret stash for yourself) and let Joan get the hint. Same for milk and other necessities. Insist she comes shopping with you for foodstuffs, and inform her on the way that you'll be splitting the bill.

The second issue is guilt. Family members can really play the 'but you're my sister' card. Or your parents may expect it of you – after all, you're the only family little Joanie has in the big city. Don't fall for it. It's one thing to help someone down on her luck, but it's quite another to become her doormat. You'll know which one you are. Try to establish how long he or she will be staying with you. As the date approaches make some gentle inquiries as to how the evacuation plan is coming along.

When parents come to stay

This can be very difficult if the family member isn't sister Joan but your mother. Mums feel entitled to live with you – after all (and there is some truth to this), they raised you and kept a roof over your head. But mums who need a roof and have other siblings or offspring should do the family tour. Work this out with your family members. Caring for one's parent should never fall to one family member only.

Your life

Mum or Joan aside, you still have a thriving social calendar. Even if you have the grooviest parents alive, they can cramp your style. This is not to say that a dinner party or cocktail hour cannot include them, it is just a different affair. But you may conclude that, even if they're under your roof, waking up with Bingo in your bed and Mum downstairs isn't the lifestyle you're after.

It is surprising how soon the parent-child roles return to their adolescent state when sex is involved. 'Dear, do you really think that that Bingo boy is right for you? I mean, he didn't even remove his shoes at the door . . .' Or if you do choose to spend the night's elsewhere, 'Is this how you conduct yourself? Sleeping around? You'll never get anywhere living like a harlot.'

The FG will have to lay down her own law if family guests get too interested in her welfare. Firmly inform them that you are quite capable of making these decisions and you're happy they're interested, but that they needn't worry.

Of course, there is some benefit to the FG if she is close to her family – their presence will be soothing if Bingo proves to be a lout. Mums are great for late-night cups of cocoa and a shoulder.

AGING PARENTS

Caring for parents should never fall to one child. But very often that is exactly what happens. It may be that your brother Tony is the only sibling who still lives in your home town. Or Tony is the only kid who ever really got along with your father. Dad never understood your FG-ness. Nonetheless, Tony needs help. Offer to spend time with your parent on holidays so that the caretaker gets a break.

Be involved in big decisions. Does your mum or dad need to be cared for in a professional facility? Which one? Who will pay? These questions need to be decided by all parties – don't lay it on one person because he or she is in that part of the country. You may have to get on a plane and go look at old people's homes with your sibling. It is the responsibility of all kids to take care of elderly parents. The FG gets proactive. And if you do all live in the same town, then there is no excuse for one kid to do all the caring.

Looking after an elderly parent isn't a chore. You may need to acquire new patience in coping with your new role

– a reversal of parent and child. This may be an adjustment. But it does not have to be a negative one – it should be cherished.

IN-LAWS – WHEN THEY DON'T LIKE YOU

You love your husband. He loves you. Your parents love him. His parents hate you. God knows why – you're an FG. Parents usually eat from your hand. Some chromosomal defect on their part has created a glitch in their psyches and they've taken against you. They've probably hated every woman in his life. And you just had the nerve to marry him thinking that the solidity of this move would inspire them to rethink their reaction to you. Nope. They just don't like you. Moreover, they barely hide it. When you pick up the phone, they ask, 'Who's that on the line.' When they come for dinner, they spend the evening asking after his work and his friends and ask you to pass the mashed potatoes. Things get worse when you have children. Of course, they adore their grandchildren, but they make no bones about the fact that you're doing a terrible job of being a mother. When the baby cries in their presence, they turn to you and ask, 'Why is he crying?' As if they already know the answer: you're his mother.

Your husband absolutely must take a stand in this situation. Of course, you can handle yourself. But as long as he doesn't acknowledge how rude they are being to you, then your hands are tied. It's more than a bit difficult for you to let them know how their behaviour makes you feel if he's carrying on as if it's normal. But remember, the way they treat you is not just a reflection of their poor opinion of you, it's a reflection of their poor opinion of him. He needs to face this. And he needs to tell them in no uncertain terms that if they want to have contact with you, him and your children, they'll

KIM IZZO *and* CERI MARSH

play nicely. You're probably never going to be close with them, but they must treat you like an adult member of the family.

Any family dynamic (you don't care for your in-laws, your parents aren't crazy about your husband) that pits husband against wife must be dealt with together. Decide that regardless of the demands put on you as individuals, you'll face it as a couple. Eventually, your cranky family members will see that they're getting nowhere with their behaviour and give it up.

How to avoid family gatherings

If you happen to live in another city, then getting out of family events is a cakewalk. But if your relatives inhabit your neighbourhood or are within commuting distance, then wangling out of Christmas or birthdays may be more tricky. If you're a known career-FG, then work is usually enough to let you off the hook. But really, you will need to be present for at least one family gathering per year. Call these command performances. Every FG will know which dinner or party is the one that she will attend lest she be disowned.

How to avoid his *family gatherings*

Many couples find it necessary to be democratic about holiday time, and to alternate which family gets the happy couple each year.

Unfortunately, the FG just doesn't always enjoy her boyfriend's/husband's family. Perhaps his parents fight the entire time, or perhaps they pick on her beau constantly. Whatever the reason, the FG finds herself daydreaming about what her own family is doing that very moment and she makes a silent pact to never spend the holiday with these people again.

Now she has to put her plan into action. For one thing she can be honest and tell her man that his relatives make her uncomfortable and ruin the holidays for her. Chances are, he too is confounded by his parents' and siblings' behaviour and so won't argue this point. You'll have to make a compromise. Suggest that next year you do a cocktail hour with his kin and then move along to yours.

Here's where it is tricky and the FG needs to be fair. He may agree to your being there only for cocktails, but when you want to move along to your folks he may insist that he stay put. You shouldn't be angry with him. He's entitled to stay with his parents, as you are to go be with yours. Even if you think his family total boors, he may enjoy them. There is no law that says couples must have Christmas or Easter dinner together. Another FG compromise is to host the holiday meal at her place. Invite both sets of parents and grandparents. Or if the FG has her own children or steps, she can tell her parents and his that she's doing her own family dinner. Keeping it small.

If you knew when you were dating that you never want to trade your family gatherings for his, then make a deal prior to engagement and marriage. Simply tell him that you don't want the traditional arrangement and that you will be spending such-and-such-a-holiday with your family and that you have no problem with him being with his. Then you can both set up a romantic late-night meal or drinks for the holiday for when you both return home.

HOW TO SURVIVE FAMILY GATHERINGS

The key to surviving family get-togethers is to remind yourself as you walk in the door that you are an adult. Family events tend to go badly when the whole family regresses to the last point in time when they all cohabited. You start acting like a seventeen-year-old and your father starts treating you like one, too. And since there are some nice features to this arrangement – there's some comfort in being babied – lots of people let it slide. The downside to family time travelling will soon become apparent and you will remember why you left in a huff after Easter dinner. You've happened to forget the broccoli, so your sister somehow uses that as an opportunity to chastise you for forgetting her birthday. Then Mum chimes in agreeing that you've always been a bit too self-absorbed ... and so on. To avert total disaster and desertion, bring up work as soon as you can fit it into the conversation. Talk about the repair you just had done to your car. Obviously, this is not the most riveting chat you can produce, but it does set a tone. Don't take the bait.

YOUR NEW COMBINED FAMILY

If an FG falls in love with a man who was previously married, she may find herself in a new and unexpected role: stepmum. If she has no children of her own, this will be particularly challenging, as her first experience at parenting is going to be tougher than the more traditional one. Once you've made a serious commitment to a man with kids, the two of you need to decide how involved you're all going to be. If you marry will the kids live with you or with their mother? These are conversations that must happen before marriage.

Biting your tongue

Fabulous Girls in general were raised in homes where manners were instilled. Obviously if her stepkids are not raised to have manners, and 'please' and 'thank you' are nary in sight, an FG will cringe every time they lumber over her threshold. But now that you're the official parent feel free to do what you couldn't when you were only the girlfriend.

Correct them! Go right ahead and say, 'You meant, "Please pass the salt."' This will drive them crazy but just because they're rude to your husband does not mean you have to be treated thus. And, quite frankly, you're only doing them a favour as rude adults are not very well received.

The stepmother FG is also free to call the kids on their behaviour. If your precious stepkid's idea for Father's Day is for you and their dad to cook them a meal while they loll on the sofa and they don't bother with a gift either, promising that it will come next time they see their dad, then it is perfectly acceptable for the FG to 'innocently' ask the very next time she sees them, 'So what did you end up getting your dad for Father's Day?'

However, the father may resent the FG's honesty. Divorce involving kids can cause parents to be consumed by guilt. So correcting or criticizing the kids will seem evil to the father. He's essentially afraid of them. Perhaps they'll like their mum better. Who knows. Chances are, he'll deny these feelings, but you as the FG will know they exist and you have to be sensitive to them.

In other words, while you're dying to exclaim the next time they visit and they're ensconced on the sofa, 'Hey, I see it's more quality time with Dad,' you may not want to risk upsetting your husband. Even though you're quite right and his kids treat him abominably, even disrespectfully, he may end up turning his frustration on you, and then you have a fight on your hands. You may have to bite your tongue to be supportive of the man you love, even if it kills you. But you don't have to indulge the kids in their slothful behaviour. If it is clear that (a) they will never help around the house and (b) your husband won't let you make them help, then as an FG you are absolutely absolved of having to join in with your husband and cook and clean for them. Just point out to your mate that you don't feel you should do everything for kids of their age – after all, they are quite capable. He should not force you or be angry – he has no right to be. Being a slave to his kids is his choice. You may find that he will begin to see the light when he sees his kids through your eyes.

Poor babies

No matter how difficult it may be to become a stepmother, and no matter how difficult your stepkids are, you must remember that they are children. The combining of families is simply harder for children than it is for adults. They are necessarily in this against their will. Even kids who get along with their stepmum would prefer it if Mummy and Daddy had stayed together – no matter what they may say. The best course of action for the newly minted stepmum is a casual one. Friendly, yes; buddy-buddy, no. Don't think that you and your new stepdaughter are going to be instant best friends and that she will pour her little heart out to you. You are, after all, part of the problem in her eyes (at least in the beginning).

If the style in which you want to run your home is wildly different from what the kids are used to, let them know what kind of changes you're going to be expecting. 'We're all going to clean up these dishes together before watching TV, actually.' You may be dying to also say, 'I'm not a maid like your mother!' But don't, unless you want to earn the title of stepmonster.

Other people's money, other people's kids

Money. Money can be a source of tension for any couple. Children – those that aren't yours – only exacerbate this. Even if you actually have a great relationship with your stepkids, money spent on them and not on you may irritate you. The truth is, if you don't have your own kids and don't want your own, then you probably made that decision because you want to live a life that is freer and includes more disposable income to spend on, well, yourself. Forget about being called shallow – this is a perfectly natural feeling. While you are not expected to contribute financially to the rearing of your husband's progeny, you are expected to accept that he does. This can mean that your hopes for a two-week trip to Italy will be dashed as you watch him send his son on some European excursion. Or that you can't put the downpayment on your dream house because he has to keep a wad of dough in safekeeping for his kid's tuition.

While the FG will applaud her husband's commitment to his offspring, she will have to make some tough decisions. If she is making good money, perhaps she may have to top off the downpayment, or pay for her husband's airline ticket to Italy. Or choose to go away with friends in lieu of a couple holiday.

I sat alone at the table for a bit trying to catch my breath. I was half expecting the waitress to come by and bring Nice back to the table, like the last course in the meal. But she didn't. It was just me. And it looked like it would just be me for a while. Then my mobile rang. I couldn't tell who it was at first, it just sounded like a wounded animal moaning. I was about to hang up when the voice became clear.

'It's me. I'm having a baby. Can you meet me in the hospital?' panted Eleanor.

'Oh, my God, Eleanor! I can be there in ten minutes. Are you okay?'

'I'm having a baby. It hadn't quite occurred to me until about half an hour ago. See you at the hospital.'

Missy picked me up in a taxi outside the restaurant and we rushed to Eleanor's side. Things were progressing quickly and Eleanor looked scared. Even though we were in one of those birthing rooms that are meant to calm everyone down, things were pretty intense. Contractions came over Eleanor like waves and she would yell as if possessed. Missy and I each held a hand and fed her ice chips between contractions but we felt as if we weren't doing nearly enough for her. Twenty-one hours of labour later and still no baby, the doctor announced that he was worried about the baby's progress and decided El would need a caesarean. He was very matter-of-fact and El took the news well, but I could tell she was scared. While they set things up for the C-section, I remembered a story I'd heard from a couple in a similar situation. The husband read stories to his wife during the operation to distract her from what was going on south of the white sheet. I excused myself, ran out to the waiting room and picked up a few magazines from the limited selection.

'Okay, Eleanor, do you want to hear about a religious conversion or shark attacks?' I held up two magazines.

'Shark attacks, definitely, I want to hear about people in worse situations than me.' I began reading, and after about twenty minutes there was a loud squack as Eleanor's baby girl took in her first breath. When they brought her over to Eleanor, I think we all felt a bit shocked that it was a real, live baby. Her head was absolutely round and her skin was pink and perfect.

'Hello, Olivia, welcome to the world.'

CHAPTER NINE

Entertaining

I called it a housewarming party, but I'd been living in my place for nearly two months before I felt I was really ready for the unveiling. I'd painted – lavender on the living-room wall looked fab! – planted a little garden and tried a few different furniture arrangements until it felt perfect for Kitty and me. And that night, with votive candles on practically every surface, my little home really shone. Eleanor and Missy came over early to help me set everything up.

I had invited Nice to the party even though we'd broken up. I'd become so used to having him in my life for the important moments that it just seemed wrong not to ask him. He sent me an e-mail saying he didn't think he'd feel comfortable.

'Well, can you blame him?' asked Eleanor. She was polishing my wine glasses and lining them up on the kitchen island. It was her first evening away from Olivia, and so far she seemed to be holding up pretty well. She had only phoned the babysitter twice in the half-hour she'd been at my place.

'No, I understand. It just feels weird that he's not here. Maybe I shouldn't have bought this place and brought things to a head. Then we'd still be together.'

Missy shook her head, 'This place is so great. You guys would have realized that you wanted different things sooner

281

or later. Like me and Joe.'

That didn't ring true to me, but the doorbell did, so I didn't need to get into a conversation with Missy about how our relationships had nothing in common.

Soon my place was full of friends. The music was just right, everyone seemed to be laughing and mingling – and, I must say, complimenting me on my décor. Even Kitty was having a good time, weaving through everyone's legs and receiving praise for her beauty, as she always does. I'd invited every-one from my office to come, even though I wasn't feeling that close to them. I knew I had to make more of an effort with them. After all, I really needed my job now that I had a mortgage. Cheryl and Marshall showed up, but I was not surprised that Bradley didn't make it. Frank, the newspaper section editor I'd been writing for, did make an appearance though. Every time the door opened I couldn't help but hope it might be Nice. Maybe he'd changed his mind. But it never was. I went over to the bar to make sure there was still enough ice, and I came upon the thing that strikes the most fear in a hostess's heart: a gossip columnist.

There was Dudley, standing in my kitchen. How dare he show up here! He must have ducked through the door after some guests were buzzed into the building. He was as ridiculous as ever in a suit that looked as if it had come from the children's department, blue velvet with five buttons all done up and a blue satin tie knotted thickly at his throat. His nearly white hair was slicked back with grease.

I was calm. 'Dudley. I'm at a loss. How does one express displeasure at your company since you're someone who so obviously doesn't care about the feelings of others?'

'Come on, Manners Girl, what are you going to do, throw me out of your party? You'll only be forcing me to reveal you as a less-than-gracious host, now, won't you? I mean, what am I doing to deserve to be kicked out? I'm just standing here.'

'You little weasel,' I hissed.

'Ooh, that's not polite at all!'

Okay, so I wasn't keeping my cool so well. What I really wanted to do was to remove him bodily. Which would not have been so hard. I'm sure I had at least fifteen pounds on him. People had begun to notice our little fracas and were starting to whisper to each other about it. I saw that Frank, my newspaper friend, was keeping his distance but watching our argument. Dudley was ruining my night in so many ways. He leaned back smugly on the island, in a mockery of making himself comfortable. Kitty chose that moment to hop up on the island, and I swear she wrinkled her little nose at the sight of Dudley.

'The way I see it, Manners Girl, I'm in charge here. You are obliged to be polite or your reputation will be ruined, and I can do or say anything I want because . . . well, because I don't care what anyone thinks.' And with that, Dudley grinned a weasely grin and leaned back even further onto the island.

I was silenced momentarily thinking about what he'd just said. He was right – the room was full of media types. What would it look like if I made a scene and dispelled someone from my party, even if that somebody was evil Dudley? And by now half the party was watching the show.

The smoke show, that is. At first it was just was a thin plume of smoke rising from the back of Dudley's head. Then actual flames. It made him look even more devilish than usual. When Dudley realized that he was on fire, he panicked. He was genuinely afraid for his life. The fire was spreading, catching onto a stack of paper napkins and lighting up the dried flower arrangement. Everyone around us froze. The fire alarm wailed. I grabbed a pitcher of water and emptied it onto Dudley's head. Eleanor dumped the ice bucket onto the island to put out the fire there. Marshall grabbed a chenille throw and wrapped Dudley in it to further douse the flames.

'Are you okay? Let me see your back. I think it's all out,' I said, checking Dudley's burnt jacket. It was in tatters.

'You saved my life, Manners Girl.' Dudley was breathing hard, still in shock.

'You're burnt quite badly. I think you'll need to go to the hospital. Who can I call for you?'

Newspaper Frank came over then. 'I'll take him to the hospital. But will you promise to call me tomorrow?'

'Okay,' I answered. I hoped he wasn't going to try to turn this into another opportunity for me and Dudley to swing at each other in print. It wasn't fun anymore.

He must have read my mind, for he said, 'It's not about a story. It's about a job. Call me, I'll be in early.' And with that, Frank whisked Dudley, tatters and all, out of my home.

Entertaining

The Fabulous Girl will always be up for a good time, whether she's having a few friends over to watch a movie or attending another's eleven-course meal. An FG knows that preparation is key to entertaining well. She thinks – in advance – about what will please her guests and goes out of her way to make her parties stylish and fun. Even when she is simply a guest, an FG understands that she should be making a contribution. She arrives at the right time, dressed nicely and in the mood to socialize. But no amount of forward thinking can ward off the unexpected or even disastrous events that can occur at social events. There are times when an FG must cope with hostess hijinks and entertain by the seat of her pants.

How to Prepare Yourself for . . .

A DINNER PARTY YOU ARE THROWING

Have your apartment ready (lights dimmed, CD playing, food mostly prepared, table set) and be dressed and made up. In fact, change into your hostess outfit at least fifteen minutes before you are expecting guests to arrive. Pour yourself a glass of wine to sip as you prepare dinner.

A DINNER PARTY YOU ARE ATTENDING

We all know that it's worse to show up early than late to a dinner party. If the invitation was for 7:30, your hosts are almost certainly not ready at 7:30. And they are expecting to serve drinks before ushering everyone to the table. It's perfect to arrive about fifteen minutes late to a dinner party.

If you have some legitimate reason for being much later than that (a car accident, an act of God), then you must call to warn your hosts. Even if your hosts weren't planning to start serving dinner until 8:30, if you arrive at 8:25 then you've just made the last hour an anxious one for them. If you are the hostess and one or two guests are quite late, you should only hold things up for them for a limited time. Never let the cocktail hour last longer than an hour – momentum will be lost, sobriety will be lost and so on. Whenever it is that the stragglers arrive, they should sit down and just join the dinner at whatever point it's at, be it first, second or third course.

A COCKTAIL PARTY YOU ARE ATTENDING

When your beau comes to pick you up, pour each of you a quick drink. A shot of vodka (which you keep in the freezer) with a twist of lime will give you a bit of fire and can barely be detected on your breath.

A BLACK-TIE EVENT

Choose and try on your gown at least forty-eight hours before the event. There may need to be alterations. There is nothing more vexing than to have a custom-made dress sent to your home hours before the party only to discover it's not what you expected and now you must attend the do looking like Cruella DeVille.

A SPORTING EVENT

Don't try to one up the rest of the hardcore fans and competitors by turning up at the horse show in stilettos. You may think you'll outshine everyone, but in fact you'll look silly. Research whatever type of sport you're going to see. Is it sailing? Football? Cricket? Polo? Surfing? And add your own brand of chic to the proper attire.

A WORK EVENT

Chances are you're going straight from the office. Give yourself an extra half-hour to freshen up. Take your FG-at-work supplies to the ladies', brush your teeth, reapply your lipstick and fluff your hair. This break between your desk and whatever reception it is you're headed to allows you to switch gears. Even though this is a work-related party, you still want to have a bit more energy than the third-quarter report required. Once you arrive, head to the ladies' to give yourself a final look in the mirror, straighten shirts or jackets and so on before entering the actual room. This five-minute prep will make you more confident and you'll appear unflustered. And remember not to drink too much!

Last-Minute Entertaining

You're home after a long day at work. The suit is off and the sweat-pants are on. You're flaked out on the couch eating a bag of crisps and thinking how nice your night will be. Your sweetheart will come home, get comfortable, and maybe the two of you will rent a movie and order in. And then the call comes: 'I'm so sorry, I forgot to tell you I've invited my boss over for dinner. We'll be there in half an hour.' Of course, at some later point there will be a conversation about how wrong it is to put a girl in this position. A *long* conversation. But for now you have half an hour to pull a dinner party out of thin air.

Tell Mr Lucky-to-be-with-the-Sweetest-Woman-Alive to

bring home some wine. Then turn your attention to food. If your kitchen and pantry is even halfway stocked, you can do it. Pasta is the easiest route. Who has four steaks in the fridge? Nobody, that's who. Get a sauce going. Don't worry if you have to start with a bottle of ready-made, you can jazz it up. Sauté some garlic and onion and whatever other vegetables (mushrooms, peppers, celery) you've got and have cut quite fine. And the bottle of sauce. Throw in a bit of dried chilli. While the sauce is doing its thing, look around your place. Clear the clutter, don't clean. Look more carefully at the bathroom, wipe down the counter, pull the shower curtain closed. Now get changed into something presentable in case they show up even a minute early. Put on some music. Light the candles. Pour them stiff drinks as soon as they walk in the door.

HINTS FOR IMPROMPTU DINNERS

The food
To pull off even a modest dinner party on next to no notice, you need a pantry stocked with the basics:

- Garlic
- Onions
- Dry pasta
- Rice
- Potatoes
- Butter
- Milk
- Tinned tomatoes and mushrooms
- Tomato and mushroom soups in cans
- A jar of decent ready-made pasta sauce
- Capers
- Black olives

- Lemons and limes (or even the bottled-juice variety)
- Grated Parmesan
- A pepper mill
- Salt
- Tabasco and worcestershire sauces
- A variety of dried herbs and spices: oregano, basil, parsley, paprika, ginger, dried chilli flakes, rosemary and thyme

The drink

An FG knows the importance of a stocked bar. It allows her to be a more spontaneous hostess since she's not starting from scratch with her drinks cabinet every time she thinks of having friends over. When you have the basics in your bar – red and white wine, vodka, gin, whiskey, vermouth, brandy and bitters – it feels like less of an outlay when you want to start adding to it. You might be entertaining a friend whom you know has very specific tastes. Your boyfriend may get an unexpected promotion. An FG starts to add to her basic bar:

- Champagne
- Single-malt scotch
- Bourbon
- Cointreau
- Grappa (which may be kept in the freezer) and other liqueurs
- Pernod
- Port

How to Build a Guest List

The guest list is the most important ingredient for any successful party. Of course, you'll invite some of your close friends, but you should include those you don't know well.

Perhaps they are friends or people you've chatted with briefly at an event; either way, don't be shy when extending invitations and don't worry that these groovy new people won't want to attend – just ask.

Wine

WHINING ABOUT WINE

Of course, as the Fabulous Girl develops her culinary skills and as her pocketbook grows, she may become choosier with the wine she serves with meals and therefore not rely on her guests to provide the libations. (Many 'sophisticated' social types wince at the thought of opening up a guest's bottle, but for many younger people, if guests don't bring wine, there may not be any at all.) If your guests do bring wine, you can add these bottles to your 'cellar.' The wine is a gift to the hostess and you are not compelled to open it that evening. Even if a guest who fancies himself a connoisseur insists that the Reisling he bought is just killer with rack of lamb, you do not have to open it. But if he does not let up, it may be easier to do so. There's nothing more tedious than an overly long discussion about wine.

BETTER DEAD THAN RED

If as a guest you have a nasty or unpleasant reaction to a certain type of wine, then you should inform your hosts in advance and let them know that you will happily bring your own bottle so as not to put them out. As a host in this situation, you can, depending on your budget, decline this offer or accept it graciously. But if for some reason you've neglected to tell the host of your allergy or problems with migraines you should graciously refuse the wine rather than suffer. If an alternative is not presented, then be content to sip on another beverage.

Dinner Parties with Vegetarians and Vegans

More and more people are adopting alternative eating habits. Vegetarians are now common, and vegans, who don't consume any animal products, including things such as cheese and eggs, are also becoming more prevalent. Of course this can mean some fancy foot-work for a hostess.

If you invite either V type to your dinner party ensure you have enough meat-free food for them. Do not ask them over and then insist that they bring their own dish so as not to inconvenience you. If it's dinner then feed them like the other guests.

Likewise, if you are a V girl, you should not accept a dinner party invite then get either (a) vocally squeamish at the meat or (b) self-righteous with the other guests about your choice. Understandably however, many V's prefer to not have their vegetable delight cooked on the same grill as meat. If your host has only one BBQ, then you must bring your own small Hibachi. As the host, please inform your V guests that they are welcome to eat animal-free but that you only have the one BBQ.

Pot-luck

This type of entertaining runs from the casual 'having the girls over to watch *Sex and the City*' to the more formal, 'Cousin Claire is getting married again.' We all know the rules: the host calls around and with pen and paper writes down everyone's contribution. The more organized will even give out the assignments: Jenny brings the salad, Bob the cheese plate and so on. Invariably there will be those who turn up with a store bought fill-in-the-blank. And those who have slaved over their bean salad will tsk-tsk the one with the frozen strawberry cheesecake. With everyone being so busy these days, we can safely cut slack to those who choose to shop not chop. It may not taste as good as your own homemade miracle, but as long as you all did your parts then it's okay. Especially since not everyone is adept in the kitchen – the shopper may actually be sparing you. And please refrain from making repeated jabs at the person who hasn't cooked. Just eat.

Fake Dinner-Party Invites

The FG gets the phone call inviting her to a dinner party next week at a friend's. She arrives looking fabulous, bottle of wine in hand. Her hosts open the door looking less fabulous, the house not quite clean, and then sit the FG down on the sofa and casually offer her a variety of takeaway menus. 'We thought we'd just get delivery.' This is a far-too-common occurrence.

There is absolutely nothing wrong about ordering in food. If you know that your Indian food is never going to be as good as your favourite restaurant's, then by all means call up and order their *aloo gobi*. Order in advance and decide when you'd like it delivered. Set a lovely table just as you would if you were making it yourself.

If you decide to go this route, the invitation should come with that caveat. Miscommunication is impolite. And as a host, if you choose to surprise your guests with takeout, be prepared to pay for it yourself. If you pay with a credit card over the phone you'll avoid the uncomfortable moment when the food arrives and everyone reaches for their wallets.

Likewise, do not have people over for 'dinner' then announce that you'll all be walking over to the Italian restaurant down the street. People think that an invitation to dinner means you'll be cooking. If this is not the case, give fair warning.

If as a guest, you're now poring over a Thai menu when you had imagined you'd be sitting down to a homemade meal, just go with it. Sulking does not become the Fabulous Girl. While it's not acceptable to chastise your takeaway-loving friends, it is fine to mention that you'll need to run out to the nearest ATM before the food arrives.

Odd Girl Out

When you're having dinner with colleagues, you probably do the same thing – everyone tends to talk shop. It's fun. You want to know what everyone is up to, who got which new job, who is about to get the sack and so on. This is perfectly acceptable behaviour – unless. Unless you are in mixed company. It is never polite to talk at length on subjects from which any one person in the social group is excluded. This isn't to say that a subject should be banned, but the way it's discussed must be considered. If you realize that Bingo is the only non-dentist at the dinner party then you may draw him into the conversation: 'When we were in school we had the most evil professor named Dr Molar. Really, that was his name . . .' Even still, be aware of how long you are lingering on a subject that Bingo can contribute nothing to or cannot even ask anything about.

If you find yourself the odd man out at a dinner party – at a cocktail party you can simply wander off to another

KIM IZZO *and* CERI MARSH

conversational circle – there are a few things you can do. First, assume that because you come from a different field or background you are actually the most interesting person in the room. This group is probably sick of having the same old conversation and is just dying to have someone throw out a new opinion. You can either start with one of the people sitting on either side of you or take on the whole table. Granted, this is a bold gambit, but it's one that could really make the party – and your reputation as a desirable dinner guest. If you're going to go for it, you should lead with something everyone will relate to or have an opinion about. A book that's on the bestseller list. A film that people are likely to have seen. A world event. 'Is it just me, or is the new show at the National Gallery the worst exhibition of the last ten years? An obvious money grab!' Even if only half the people at the table have seen the show, the ones who haven't will be drawn into the new conversation.

Duelling Hosts

You've heard that their dinner parties get lively, but you weren't expecting this. Bingo and Fifi have served up the main course and now they're serving up the ugliest secrets of their marriage. You hadn't noticed, but maybe Fifi consumed rather a lot of wine during the first course and that jokey little back-and-forth during the cocktail hour about which of them was supposed to have picked up the groceries needed for dinner actually had more teeth than you had first guessed. Now they're bringing his parents into it, and that last family trip they took together. Who had paid for it in the end? Who? Well, Fifi had ended up putting down her credit card when Bingo's cheapskate father had choked. And there you are, a table of silenced ping-pong watchers.

Sometimes all that's needed is for someone to gently draw the couple's attention to the fact that they've crossed the line. When this doesn't work, stronger measures are called for. The evening is pretty much shot anyway, so you may as well barge in: 'Okay, you two, maybe you should finish this a little later when it's just the neighbours who will have to listen?' If even this tactic doesn't stop the deluge, then you could suggest that the rest of the group pick up their drinks and move into the living room. Or you could simply get up and leave.

Co-host

Entertaining is a stressful proposition, even for those with a lot of practice. You want to do it well, and so you have a lot on your mind. The last few minutes before the doorbell rings can be the most tense of all. Is the music on? The table set? The wine decanting? Even though this work is halved by the presence of a mate, somehow the potential for agitation is doubled. Be aware of this strange entertaining equation and make a decision to remain on the same team as your co-host/spouse. There's nothing worse for your guests than arriving at your door to feel the tension between the two of you. A good way to avoid getting on each other's nerves is to get out of each other's way. Divide and conquer the work. She sets and decorates the table, he oversees salad and main.

He's gone too far

You love his quirks. You don't even mind his unsubstantiated diatribes on the superiority of Korean cars. But this time he's out of line. Yesterday's conversation about whether or not the two of you are going to have kids is suddenly bubbling up in the most unappealing way during dessert. It takes you a moment to focus on what he's saying to his dining neighbours, and then you hear it: 'I don't even like children. I don't understand the desire for them – it's kind of sick to me, actually.' Of course, this display of his is pure aggression toward you. It's nasty and childish. Nevertheless, you are the hostess of the dinner party where it is all unravelling and so you must buck up and get through it. Even in this extreme situation you may not start channelling a *Who's Afraid of Virginia Woolf?*-style aggression and throw crystal at his head. Hopefully your man will respond to the look of death that you are shooting at him from across the table – although he is showing himself to be a most insensitive sort – and shut up. If not, then you must dive into conversation with the people sitting next to you and ignore him for the rest of the night. Well, at least until your guests leave.

How to Host the Famous

If you know people who are well known (be it a Hollywood actor or your town's mayor), you may have occasion to integrate them with your more modestly accomplished friends. How you handle this situation depends on how well adjusted the famous person is to his fame. In the best-case scenario, the famous pal is well adjusted and has no trouble moving among civilians. With this kind of friend it's easy to throw them into any kind of entertaining. Your other guests may have a moment upon entering the room of 'Oh, my God, is that really *the* Bingo Jones?' Then Bingo's relaxed manner will put them at ease and they'll soon be mingling comfortably. If, on the other hand, Bingo is self-conscious about his profile – which unfortunately can manifest in the deforming belief that everyone wants something from the well known – then small groups may be a better way to go. A dinner party, say, where Bingo can become comfortable with a smaller group and no one is making any sudden movements to scare him. The only downside to this is that by the end of the night, Bingo will probably dominate the conversation and want to feel that the other guests are basking in his glow. A bit of a bore, but either way all your guests will remember it as a fascinating evening.

When the Hostess Gets Sick in the Middle of the Party

You're having a lovely time at a dinner party. The meal is finished, and people are standing around the hostess's comfortable apartment. The guy you've had your eye on for months is telling you all about his trip to Paris – his parents have an apartment on the Île de la Cité and he goes at least once a year. Suddenly you notice your hostess bolt for the bathroom looking a bit green. And she stays there. And stays there. Although you don't want to pull yourself away from the conversation you're in ('You should see this apartment, it looks right over Shakespeare & Co . . . Do you ever get to Paris?'), you know you really should check on your friend. As discreetly as you can, extract yourself from the party, knock gently on the door and enquire after her health. If she tells you she's fine, then leave her alone. Let her know, however, that you could fetch her some Aspirin or a glass of water, whatever she may need in there.

If she's really ill – puking her guts out – then be willing to go into hostess mode yourself. Find out what she wants you to do and then just do it. Does she want you to just tend to her party while she pulls herself together? In this case you don't have to organize a game of charades, just listen for the end of the CD, refresh drinks and so on. Or would she like you to clear everyone out of her place? Whatever it is, do it with the least amount of fuss. She probably feels ridiculous on top of feeling ill and so doesn't want a lot of attention drawn to the situation. If you do have to boot everyone out of her place politely, you should be the last person to leave. Make sure she has everything she needs – and make sure it's not so serious that she needs a trip to the hospital or for you to run out to an all-night pharmacy. Quickly stack up the dinner plates so she doesn't wake up to an utter disaster, and then be off. And, of course, call the next day to find out if she's feeling better. Assure her that in every other way, the night was a delight.

Food Poisoning

FGs love dinner parties – it's the social occasion where they shine most brightly. And hosts love FGs for the same reason. A host knows she can count on an FG to add to the conversation and fun of the evening. An FG can handle almost any bump in the road that comes her way during a dinner party. Including bad dinner. Obviously all dinner-party hosts are not gourmet chefs, and most well-mannered people can make it through a bland pasta or an overly seasoned soup. But what's an FG to do if she bites into a mouthful of baby greens sprinkled with walnuts that have turned rancid? Or worse, if she's served a skewer of raw chicken?

It is not in the least ill mannered to save yourself from food poisoning in these situations. If you know your hostess well and the group at the table is made up of good friends, you should just speak up. Be as friendly and light as possible: 'Fifi, your timer must be broken because I think you meant to cook this chicken a little longer.' And then immediately help Fifi – who will of course be mortified – deliver the chicken sushi back to the kitchen for a little more time on the grill. A good hostess would rather suffer a moment's embarrassment than send all her guests to the hospital. If you don't know your hostess well or if the dinner is a more formal one, do whatever you can to get her out of the room with you: 'Fifi, could I trouble you for some Aspirin?' Once you're out of earshot, you can gently let her know about the raw chicken.

If You Hate the Food

Perhaps the side dish or the main isn't rancid but just plain unpalatable? Try to stomach as much of the dish as you can, and try moving the food around your plate so it appears to have been eaten. Then simply put your utensils down. If your host asks you point blank if you didn't enjoy her braised sweetbreads, say that it was fine but you're just full.

If Someone Catches on Fire or Chops Off a Finger, and Other Disasters

Your host has served a lovely meal. He knows he's brought an interesting group of people together. He's made his apartment warm and inviting by covering every surface with candles. As the group gets up from the table to sip after-dinner drinks, he leans back against his mantelpiece, resting an elbow there while telling a story. Then you notice the smoke. The arm of Bingo's shirt – no, actually, Bingo's arm – is on fire. Everyone freezes. Someone shouts at Bingo to roll on the ground. The fire is moving up his sleeve. Bingo is frozen in fear. The FG springs into action, grabs a bottle of sparkling mineral water off the table and pours it over Bingo.

KIM IZZO *and* CERI MARSH

The fire is out. If Bingo's burns are serious enough to warrant a trip to the hospital – and they probably are – the FG offers him her company while he waits in the emergency room. Whether or not Bingo takes her up on her offer, the FG follows up the next day to check up on his injuries and to thank him for the party. Many people feel awkward in these situations and fear that Bingo may not want to receive calls after such an evening. But nothing could be further from the truth. The absence of such a call will be perceived as lack of concern for his health.

Dinner Is Ruined

You read the recipe wrong. The oven was supposed to be set at 350 degrees for 45 minutes, not 450 degrees for 35 minutes. The chicken is now black on the outside and raw on the inside. And your guests have not even sat down yet. You need to quickly take stock of the situation. Can your first course be added to in a way that will make it a main course? A green salad could be turned into a niçoise with a tin of tuna and the potatoes that were going to go with the chicken. If no such shift can be made, then go ahead and serve the appetizer as you'd planned. But before you do, call up a good Indian or Thai restaurant and order in the rest of the meal. You needn't even say anything about it until the doorbell rings. Everyone will laugh and remember how unflappable you were in this little crisis.

She Went Out with Him?

Even after a lot of thoughtful planning, an FG can realize she's blundered once it's too late. As the guests are arriving, you spot a snarl at the coatrack. And then another guest lets you in on the problem: Tom and Yvette were once – years and years ago – a couple. Yvette had an affair, the end was messy and Tom has never fully recovered. Now they are in your home with their respective dates and you feel bad. The only thing to do is to assume the best in your friends, that they will be able to handle the evening with a little support from you. Don't fuss over them or shoot them I'm–sorry looks all night. Quickly rethink whatever seating plan you had in mind. Obviously, you are going to want to separate them as much as possible. And make sure that during the cocktail hour you tell each of them how fantastic they look.

Who to Invite?

You were close friends with both halves of the couple and you felt badly when they split. You don't want to have to choose which of them you carry on a friendship with, and you shouldn't have to. But you do have to be sensitive to how you handle invitations to them. Don't try mixing them together at parties for at least six months if your friends' relationship was a serious one. It's a rare broken-up couple who will want to be invited to a dinner party together but separately. Cocktail parties are the place where you can pull off simultaneous invitations. You should, however, warn your friends of your plans. Don't make a big deal of it, just let them know: 'I'd love it if you could make it on Saturday night. Just so you know, I've also invited Nathan.' You do have to be prepared for the possibility that your friend is not ready to be at a party with her ex and will pass on your party. Don't give her a hard time. Never make a friendship contest out of an issue like this. It's not about you.

Coupledom

A couple joined by love and or marriage is not a single entity. However, within their social circle, they are connected for obvious reasons. So what do you do when you only care for one part of a couple? Even if you don't necessarily hate Bingo's wife, you may simply feel closer to him and prefer his company solo. Of course, you may actually loathe one half of said couple. While you're not obliged to become best buddies with Fifi, there are rules of etiquette for the treatment of a couple that you only care for half of.

DINNER PARTIES

It is never acceptable to invite only one-half of a couple to a dinner party. You can, though, seat the half of the couple you are less interested in at the far end of the table.

COCKTAIL PARTIES OR CASUAL DRINK GET-TOGETHERS

Again, you must invite both parts of a couple. A good rule of thumb when considering making this kind of half-invite is to imagine telling your mate that you'll be going out to a social function on Saturday but he's not invited. How well would that go over?

Except

Obvious exceptions to these rules must be made for work, club or single-gendered groups. If Fifi and her female reading group go out once a month for dinner then she should not feel bad leaving Bingo at home. Bingo probably won't mind either.

OUTINGS AND ACTIVITIES

You and your good friend Bingo share a love of art. In fact, this mutual interest makes up a good deal of your friendship. You are not obligated to invite Bingo's wife along on your weekly gallery trips. Likewise, if you want Fifi to join your tennis tournament, you needn't feel you have to ask Bingo if he's never expressed an interest in the sport.

CONVERSATION

You bump into your friend Fifi at a cocktail party and, unfortunately for you, she is with her boorish mate Bingo. Although you could not care less if you never heard another sound from his mouth, you must take a stab at polite conversation with Bingo. It is childish and rude to address your party chit chat only to Fifi. Even if you only run into Fifi, you must ask after Bingo – pretending he doesn't exist is unacceptable.

WHAT CAN I DO?

If you find yourself and not your mate invited to something that your mate really should be included in, you must either politely insist that your loved one will be joining you or else decline the invitation altogether. Anyone who makes a point of excluding your mate from social events where he should be welcome is snubbing you both.

SNUBBING

If you do despise Fifi but for whatever reason maintain a relationship with Bingo, then you cannot snub Fifi in public. Greeting Bingo but ignoring Fifi is not acceptable.

Joint snubbing

If you are the victim of a snub then your partner should not go out of his way to be friendly with the snubber as this only encourages the behaviour. If you are the partner then be sympathetic and perhaps next time the ill-mannered lout selects you for the snub, employ the useful 'nicing' tactic and force the snubber to say hello to both of you.

YOU AND YOUR EX

There are times when certain members of an FG's social set won't like the man in her life. Not everyone in your life has to like each other. But how do you handle it if these ambivalences result in the absence of invitations? It's perfectly acceptable to maintain friendships with someone you used to date, even if he and your current beau aren't crazy about each other. You do have to be careful about the kind of invitations you accept from this person, however. It's fine to meet for coffee or drinks one on one, and it's also fine to go out in a group with your ex as long as your boyfriend is welcome as well. You can't agree to go out with your ex and a group of people if your boyfriend is not welcome. And if your ex is so uncomfortable with your current beau, then it may be time to re-evaluate his friendship. Is your ex really over his feelings for you? Maybe you are quietly torturing him with your friendship.

One Last Piece of Advice

There always appears to be a strange kind of guilt that arises around a party or get-together when the last morsel of snack is left on the plate. Perhaps women don't want to appear 'piggish' by eating the last spring roll or skewer of shrimp, but the Fabulous Girl knows this is silly. In fact, if the FG is eyeing that final canapé, then she does the right thing and announces to those around her, 'Does anyone else want this before I indulge?' Then she will either split it or eat it. This is perfectly mannered.

The party broke up once the fireman arrived.
They looked around to make sure everything was okay and
then headed out the door. Eleanor asked if we could go for
a ride on the truck but you could tell the firemen were used
to dealing with frisky women. And off they went.

The buzzer rang again.

'Maybe the firemen changed their minds,' said Eleanor
hopefully.

'Yeah, right,' I said. 'Hello? Nice? Hi, come up!'

I wasn't sure what to think. I was at once nervous and
elated that Nice was at this very moment coming up to see
me. The girls quickly got their things together and promised to call to check on me later. They both insisted that
they'd had a really good time until the fire started.

When I opened the door, Nice looked a little nervous
himself. I told him what had happened and showed him
around.

'You were right, it's an amazing place. You did very well.'

Which was very sweet given the state of the place. There
were puddles of water everywhere, bits of burnt fabric
floated in the puddles and the general debris from the party
cluttered the room.

'Thank you. I really wanted you to see it. It was so
strange not to have you here tonight. It seemed wrong.'

'I was wrong,' said Nice. 'I was wrong to push you about

moving in together. I just felt hurt and insulted, and I thought you were sort of breaking up with me by getting this place on your own.'

'I know, I know. And I can see why it seemed like that to you. But I wasn't. I just needed to do this. It felt really good buying this place on my own. Except I hate that you're gone.'

'I'm not gone. I mean, I'm back. Can we go back? And we'll wait until you're ready to move in together.'

And then there was the true housewarming.

Fabulous Girl Epilogue

There are a few concepts that the Fabulous Girl needs to understand in order to make the most of her great big life.

DON'T WHINE

It is very easy to slip into complaint mode. Life can be very, very stressful and very, very busy. The little things can get to us – the too-slow queue at the supermarket, the skirt that has sold out of your size, the phone bill that's too high – even more than the bigger issues. But it is very unbecoming to be a whiner. Everything in life is going badly to this person, and even the teeniest deviation from their plan seems to them to be a personal attack. The Fabulous Girl will not allow herself to fall into this pattern, and if she does, she will take steps to curb chronic complaining. If she doesn't, people will get sick of her and be afraid to ask how she is doing.

STAND UP

Of course complaints do have their purpose. The Fabulous Girl prides herself on being civil to others, but 'decorum,' as we said, doesn't mean doormat. If she's treated unfairly or not getting what she paid for, then she speaks up. Politely, of course. It's all in the tone. An FG knows how to make her point in a direct way without sounding bitter. She knows it's the more civilized – and effective – way to assert herself.

KNOW WHEN TO WALK AWAY

A Fabulous Girl can be a real trooper. Her inclination is to stick things out no matter what. A bad relationship, a horrid job, a tricky family situation. Whatever the problem, sometimes it is smarter to give up. The FG does not relish banging her head against a brick wall. But being loyal, optimistic and a hard worker, she may fancy that walking away from a problematic situation and admitting that something she cared for is over makes her a failure.

It does not. It makes her wise. There will be times in her life where there is no other option. Her mental and even physical health may depend on her leaving a negative circumstance behind. As tough as this may be, the FG can look forward to the inevitable feeling of relief that is sure to wash over her when her new-found freedom finally sinks in.

CHANGE YOUR MIND

At a certain point in her life, a Fabulous Girl may feel like she should have a comprehensive approach to life. Her life experiences will add up to a sensibility. She may know how much work means to her and decide how much to devote herself to it. She may find purpose in a rich family life and dedicate herself to that. But another thing can happen, too: She may change her mind. Her dream of getting married could be coming true, when she realizes it doesn't feel like she thought it would. She may have clocked serious hours at her career but suddenly feels like all she wants is to be home baking pies.

You've been planning to move to Paris for the past year and as the date approaches you are filled with dread rather than excitement. You probably feel as if everyone will think you're a loser or a coward by not following through. But it won't be them lying on a small bed in Paris crying from homesickness. Life's like that. It takes a great deal of courage to admit to yourself and the people close to you that you've changed your mind.

There's the old adage that it's a woman's prerogative to change her mind. The FG knows this is in fact true. So whether she decides at the last minute to call off her wedding or simply that after six months of driving a compact car trades it in for a Jeep, she has the courage to make changes she knows to be right. The FG must stand up for herself and not let the opinions or perceived opinions of others guide her beyond her own carefully considered decisions.

WRONG DECISIONS

Actually, there is no such thing as a wrong decision. An FG will learn something valuable from every outcome. Part of being an adult is taking responsibility for your actions – even the actions that don't work out in your favour. You have to allow yourself to fail but not let the possibility of failure prevent you from taking chances.

Burnout

Too many FGs feel exhausted, stressed and overworked. There comes a point in every FG's life when she must take stock and reevaluate her priorities. Things such as getting a regular good night's sleep, healthy diet and exercise should be no-brainers. But as any FG knows, work and other pressures can make these basics seem too time-consuming and she ends up neglecting one or all three. Don't work so hard that you haven't time for your friends and family, to see a film or read a novel or just to walk the dog. If you find yourself answering 'Busy' to the question 'How are you?' every time it's posed, you need to take note. So much of an FG's sense of self comes from her accomplishments at work. Couple that with a busy social life and the whole thing starts to feel like a grind. It takes real effort to scale back. Back off on some commitments and find out what it means to really get a life.

Fabulous fun

In keeping with avoiding burnout, every Fabulous Girl should commit to enjoying herself. A party, a vacation or lunch with Mum, the FG should indulge herself in things that are fun for her. After all, it's fun being a Fabulous Girl.

'I'd love it if you'd come over to my place later,' I said into Nice's voice mail. 'I'm just meeting Miss and El for dinner, but I'm sure I'll be home around 9:30 or so.'

As I walked into Dominick's, the girls – all the girls, Missy, Eleanor and Olivia – were waiting at the table. This was a big night. Missy's divorce papers had been signed that afternoon. So understandably, she was relieved and sad and emotional.

We toasted the new chapters that we were all beginning. Frank had been good to his word and had offered me a job. It seemed that the paper had such a strong response to my manners articles that they had decided they wanted me to do a column each week. I was now officially Manners Girl. And since I could write on other subjects as well, they were going to hire me on full time. I was elated. Working at *Smack!* had been a great experience, but it was obviously time to move on.

Eleanor was feeling confident about single motherhood. She was going to be away from work for a few more months, but she'd started to interview nannies and seemed to have found a good one. Missy was happily ensconced in my old apartment and beginning to talk about dating again. Everything seemed pretty perfect.

'Well, at least I'm still rich,' said Missy, taking a big gulp of her wine. Eleanor and I raised our eyebrows at each other. 'What? What's wrong with that? If it was my money when we were married, why shouldn't it be my money now?'

'I guess so,' I mumbled. Just then Olivia started fussing. Not really full-on crying, but the whining that usually precedes it. Eleanor was trying to get her used to being out in different situations. Sometimes it went smoothly, other times Olivia decided she'd had enough as soon as they arrived.

'I mean, I was supportive of Joe in our marriage. I threw dinner parties and stuff.' Missy was getting defensive. Olivia was getting testy herself. Again Eleanor and I just nodded. 'Eleanor, why is she crying? Is she hungry or something? Isn't there something you can do?'

Tears welled up in Eleanor's eyes. 'Sometimes I just don't know why she's crying. She just cries. She's a baby. I don't know what to do.' Now Eleanor was really crying.

'Oh, don't you start being a baby,' snapped Missy. 'Don't you think she should take Olivia outside?'

'That's not fair, is it?'

I sat back and watched my two best friends bicker. Although I felt bad for El (and for Olivia and Missy, too), I had another thought. Given all my friends and their crazy lives and me and my crazy life, I was never going to run out of material for my new column. So at least I had job security.

Acknowledgements

We'd like to thank the incomparable Anne McDermid and also Nathan Whitlock and Kelly Dignan; the entire Transworld team (who know how to host a fabulous office cocktail party), particularly Diana Beaumont, Emma Dowson and Patrick Janson-Smith; in Canada, the Anchor team, particularly Maya Mavjee, Martha Kanya-Forstner, Scott Richardson and Scott Sellers; Stephanie Fysh, the sweetest copy editor alive; Roxanna Bikadoroff for once again bringing the Fabulous Girl to life; to the staff at *FASHION* Magazine for their friendship and support; to the staff of *FLARE* magazine for their ongoing support, particularly Suzanne Boyd for her friendship and encouragement, and Ying Chu for rescuing the manuscript from behind locked doors one late night; the FGs for their extremely fabulous example: Lynn Creighton, Leanne Delap, Tammy Eckenswiller, Rebecca Eckler, Carole Hines, Victoria Jackman, Laura Keogh, Kate Mayberry, Leah McLaren, Caryn Mackay, Jane Miller, Tralee Pearce, Elizabeth Renzetti, Martha Sharpe, Susie Sheffman, Alex Tigchelaar, Vivian Vassos, and Victoria Winter; Kim's mother and grandmother, Carolynne Nelson and Muriel Farrell; Margaret and Trevor Northeast, David, Debbie, Dylan and Gareth Marsh for their love and support; and those indispensable FBs: Angel David, Daniel Foster, Mark Kingwell, Claude Laframboise, Lindsay Mahon, Alexander

Nagel, Doug Saunders, Russell Smith, Arlen J. Vranic and Doug Wallace; and Richard Hay for his love, patience and inspiration.

THE FABULOUS GIRL'S GUIDE TO DECORUM
by Kim Izzo and Ceri Marsh

'You know the Fabulous Girl, don't you? She's Holly Golightly, the girl you must have at your cocktail party. She's smart, fun, sophisticated, and of course beautifully well-mannered. She's the friend who always knows when you need a shoe-shopping expedition to lift your spirits. She's the one who calls you after your disastrous dinner party and insists that she had a marvellous time. She's the girl you admire, the girl you want to be.'

The Fabulous Girl's Guide to Decorum is an entertaining, stylish and thoroughly modern guide to manners. It offers invaluable advice on workplace etiquette and how to maintain the admiration and respect of your colleagues, entertaining (including how to throw the perfect dinner party and what to do if it all goes horribly wrong), sex and romance (which we all know aren't necessarily the same thing), dealing with one-night-stands, modern marriage *and* divorce, friendship and fashion. Woven throughout this wealth of witty advice is the story of the Fabulous Girl herself as she learns to glide gracefully through her days.

The Fabulous Girl's Guide to Decorum is as essential as a little black dress – elegant, practical and something no woman of today should be without!

'No woman should be without this stylish and fun guide to modern manners . . . this book is indispensable'
OK!

'The Fabulous Girl is the girl you want to be – smart, fun, sophisticated. This entertaining guide will show you how'
Heat

'Every woman should have a copy'
Woman's Own

'Don't leave home without it'
Tracey Cox, TV presenter and author of *Hot Sex*

0 552 14938 1

HOT RELATIONSHIPS
How to have one
by Tracey Cox

'Do not even attempt to fall in love or stay in love without this book'
Cosmopolitan

Are you madly in love or driven mad by it? Happily single or looking for a partner? Living together, married with kids or dumped and desperate? Whatever the state of your love life, *Hot Relationships* has the answers to all your dating and relating dilemmas.

Funny, practical and refreshingly realistic, it's packed with advice on everything from flirting and flings to monogamy and marriage. There are hot tips on getting over an ex, where to meet a partner, how to spot the losers and how to breeze through that first date, as well as hints on fixing the fights, surviving jealousy and infidelity and breaking bad love habits.

A must-have manual for singles, couples, men and women, *Hot Relationships* shows you how to have one – and how to keep it that way.

From the author of the international bestseller *Hot Sex*.

0 552 14784 2

THE SECRET DREAMWORLD OF A SHOPAHOLIC
Sophie Kinsella

When the going gets tough – the tough go shopping. . .

Meet Rebecca Bloomwood.

She's a journalist. She spends her working life telling others how to manage their money.
She spends her leisure time . . . shopping

Retail therapy is the answer to all her problems. She knows she should stop, but she can't. She tries Cutting Back, she tries Making More Money. But neither seems to work. The stories she concocts become more and more fantastic as she tries to untangle her increasingly dire financial difficulties. Her only comfort is to buy herself something – just a little something. . .

Can Becky ever escape from this dream world, find true love, and regain the use of her Switch card?

The Secret Dreamworld of a Shopaholic . . . the perfect pick me up for when it's all hanging in the (bank) balance.

'I ALMOST CRIED WITH LAUGHTER'
Daily Mail

0 552 99887 7

BLACK SWAN